Praise for
Why College Matte

"Few sectors of American society face the skepticism and pressure to change with the knowledge economy like higher education. Christian higher education is not immune, which makes it important for students enrolling in Christian universities to understand why their school is different and why it matters. No one has addressed this question more succinctly and effectively than Rick Ostrander in *Why College Matters to God*. I commend this volume to anyone looking for an accessible introduction to the mission and value of higher education that is distinctively Christian."

—**Andy Chambers,** Provost and Senior Vice President for Academic Affairs, Missouri Baptist University

"Rick Ostrander's book is the best book of which I am aware for introducing students to what Christian higher education is about. It is sound and insightful in its approach, eminently clear, and engagingly written."

—**George Marsden,** author of *The Outrageous Idea of Christian Scholarship*

"The crisp, conversational quality of *Why College Matters to God* makes it remarkably accessible for college students. For all its ease of reading, the book also bears the marks of a wise grasp of the biblical and theological grounds for learning, the history of higher education, and our present cultural moment. Combining evident faith and generous understanding, Rick has given us a fabulous resource to make good Christian sense of a college education."

—**Douglas V. Henry,** Dean of the Honors College, Baylor University

"Rick Ostrander has taken the best of *Why College Matters to God* and refreshed it for a new generation of Christian college students. Students who are eager to engage the cultural challenges of our day with a solid foundation in Christ will find a number of resources to help them make their college years a fertile training ground for developing habits of thoughtful Christian leadership."

—**Trisha Posey,** Director of the Honors Scholars Program, John Brown University

WHY
COLLEGE
MATTERS TO GOD

Third Edition

WHY

COLLEGE

MATTERS TO GOD

An Introduction to Christian Learning

Rick Ostrander

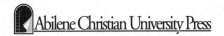
Abilene Christian University Press

WHY COLLEGE MATTERS TO GOD, 3RD EDITION
An Introduction to Christian Learning

ACU
PRESS

Copyright © 2021 by Rick Ostrander

ISBN 978-1-68426-191-8

Printed in the United States of America

ALL RIGHTS RESERVED
No part of this publication may be reproduced, stored in a retrieval system, or transmitted in any form by any means—electronic, mechanical, photocopying, recording, or otherwise—without prior written consent.

All Scripture quotations, unless otherwise indicated, are taken from the Holy Bible, New International Version®, NIV®. Copyright ©1973, 1978, 1984, 2011 by Biblica, Inc.™ Used by permission of Zondervan. All rights reserved worldwide.

Cataloging-in-Publication Data is on file at the Library of Congress, Washington, DC.

Cover design by Thinkpen Design, Inc.
Interior text design by Sandy Armstrong, Strong Design

For information contact:
Abilene Christian University Press
ACU Box 29138
Abilene, Texas 79699

1-877-816-4455
www.acupressbooks.com

22 23 24 25 26 / 7 6 5

To Lonnie,

my companion, counselor, and

soul mate throughout the adventures of life.

Contents

PREFACE TO THE THIRD EDITION

MANY years ago, I was a newly appointed dean of undergraduate studies at John Brown University in Siloam Springs, Arkansas. One of my tasks was to revamp one of those "introduction to Christian higher education" courses that Christian colleges like to inflict on their first-year students. Ours had a rather unspectacular title: "Foundations of Christian Scholarship."

Over the next two years, my colleagues and I developed a new first-year seminar that turned out to be fairly successful. One of our challenges, however, was finding a suitable textbook that covered all the relevant topics in a way that wouldn't completely bore or bewilder a first-year college student. Failing to find such a text, I wrote *Why College Matters to God*, with ample assistance from others, and Abilene Christian University Press was gracious enough to publish and promote it.

While not exactly a national best seller, *Why College Matters* did accomplish its purpose at John Brown University, and it was also adopted by several other Christian colleges and universities—mainly, I suspect, because it embodied two mantras that I seem unable to avoid as a writer: "Keep it short" and "Keep it simple." At higher education conferences, I have occasionally met attendees who see my name tag and exclaim, "Are you the guy who wrote that book we're using?" Two of our children who have participated in study abroad programs with students from other colleges have had fellow students exclaim, "Did your dad write that book that we had to read our freshman year?" I have even been surprised on occasion to discover that some institutions have used *Why College Matters* for their new-faculty orientation programs.

Twelve years have passed since *Why College Matters* first appeared, and much has changed since then. When I first wrote the book, I drew on my graduate-school texts and mentors at Notre Dame, a few years as a history professor at John Brown University, and friendships with some thoughtful Christian professors. Since then, my career path has taken me from John Brown University to a position as provost at Cornerstone University in Grand Rapids, Michigan. That job was followed by four years as vice president for the Council for Christian Colleges & Universities in Washington, DC. I now work with Acadeum, an educational-technology company based in Austin, Texas, and continue to consult for colleges and universities across the United States and the world. My work has taken me to more than eighty college campuses over the past two decades. Moreover, since the initial publication of *Why College Matters*, my wife and I have watched our four children complete degrees from five different Christian colleges.

Needless to say, much has changed in the world of college students over the past decade. There are the obvious differences in popular culture. (Sadly, in this third edition, I have to refer to *The Matrix* as a classic film that was a favorite among students' parents.) But the differences run deeper than film and music. The students for whom I wrote *Why College Matters* in the first decade of the twenty-first century were profoundly shaped by 9/11. They saw news footage of US soldiers in Afghanistan and Iraq and worried about global terrorism. Students today have had their lives disrupted by COVID-19. Perhaps they participated in protests after the murder of George Floyd, and they are entering college campuses racked by political and cultural polarization. Perhaps most importantly, students in the first decade of the 2000s were just beginning to use cell phones and computers to message friends and check Facebook, but their lives were not fundamentally shaped by electronic devices, as are the lives of students entering college today.

With so many changes in the world of college students, I was faced with the choice of bidding *Why College Matters to God* a gentle farewell or revising and updating the book. My publisher graciously consented to undertake what became not just a revision but essentially a rewrite of the original text.

So what's different about the third edition? While the reader will find the same emphasis on simplicity, clarity, and brevity, several elements have changed. Some of the changes are trivial. Film references have either been altered or explained more fully. My opening reference to *The Far Side*, that classic work of social commentary for students of my generation, has been replaced with an allusion to the novelist David Foster Wallace. More importantly, the reader will find woven into the text discussions of topics such as diversity, creation care, racial justice, and campus civility. The past decade has continued to see an increase of STEM majors, but also the continued relevance of the liberal arts, so that theme has been updated and emphasized further.

Two changes in particular deserve mention. First, I suspect that like many of my faculty peers, I tended to project my own intellectual and spiritual journey onto my students. Having moved from a childhood of believing in too many absolutes to holding fewer beliefs more tightly in my college years, I viewed college as a time in which students needed to have their beliefs critiqued, deconstructed, and reduced to a few essentials. While questioning one's beliefs is still an important aspect of college, it seems to me that for many college students today, Christian or otherwise, the primary challenge is to arrive at some key truths and values that merit their firm belief and lifelong commitment. This edition of *Why College Matters to God* subtly reflects that shift in mentality.

Second, over the past decade, both as an educator and a parent, I have gained a greater appreciation of the formative role of culture in our lives, in particular the ways that our modern culture of technology can quite literally "de-form" us as Christians. The thread of cultural resistance, therefore, runs throughout the text, and it comprises the subject of a new last chapter on living simply and living in community.

In sum, then, my hope is that the reader of the third edition will see that a primary theme of the original *Why College Matters to God*—that Christians are called to continually examine and adjust our beliefs, habits, and lives—animates not only the text of the book but the life of its author as well.

Rick Ostrander
Grand Rapids, Michigan
July 2020

Part One

Introducing the Christian College

1 CHRISTIAN WORLDVIEW AND HIGHER EDUCATION

THIS is a book for students at the start of their college years, but let's begin with a story from the other end of the college experience: commencement. Fifteen years ago at Kenyon College in Ohio, the late novelist David Foster Wallace gave what became one of the most famous commencement addresses ever. He began his talk with a well-known joke: "Two young fish are swimming along and happen to meet an older fish swimming the other way, who nods at them and says, 'Morning, boys. How's the water?' As the two young fish swim on for a bit, one of them looks at the other and says, 'What the heck is water?'"

It's not the funniest joke, but, as Foster Wallace went on to explain, it does illustrate a basic point—that the most obvious and important realities are often the ones that are hardest to notice. Or to put it another way, as modern Americans, we swim in a cultural water of assumptions, behaviors, and influences that we rarely notice and usually take for granted.

Take college, for example. A Tibetan herdsman visiting the United States would notice a strange phenomenon. Around the age of eighteen, most American young people complete a certain level of schooling known as "high school." After that, about two-thirds of them will move on to "college," where for the next four or five years, they will complete an assortment of classes that collectively make up what is called "undergraduate education."

Just what are these classes? First, they take "general education" or "core curriculum" classes such as English literature, history, natural and social sciences, and philosophy—subjects that people have been studying for centuries. Along with the core, students take classes in what they call a "major" area of study: a subject they are most interested in, or one they (or their parents) believe will yield the best career prospects. Then they fill in the rest of their courses with a minor, electives, and perhaps a study abroad program. Amid all this coursework, the students find ample time for eating, socializing, competing in athletics, and water fights in the dormitory.

It all may seem quite normal to those of us who have gone through or are going through the process. But our Tibetan herdsman probably would be hard-pressed to see the purpose in all of it. His perplexity would increase if he visited a private Christian university, where chances are students pay more money for a narrower range of academic programs and more restrictions on their social lives.

Of course, there are a variety of reasons students choose to attend a Christian college. For many, it's the perception of a safe environment. For others, it's a particular major that the school offers; or perhaps it's the Christian emphasis in the dormitories, chapel, and student organizations; or it might be the school's reputation for academic quality and personal attention from Christian professors. It may even be the prospect of finding a Christian spouse at a religious college.

None of these features, however, is unique to a Christian college. For example, if it's safety you're looking for, you could just as well attend college in Maine, which boasts the nation's lowest crime rate. Moreover, most state universities have Christian organizations on campus that provide opportunities for fellowship and ministry. One can also find good Christian professors at just about any secular university. One of the most outspoken evangelical professors I had as a college student, for example, was my astronomy professor at the University of Michigan.

The real uniqueness of a Christian college lies elsewhere. Simply stated, the difference between a Christian university and other institutions of higher education is this: a Christian college weaves a Christian worldview into the entire fabric of the institution, including academic life. It is designed to educate you as a whole person and help you flourish in every part of your life as a follower of Christ. This statement will take a while to unpack in all its complexity, and that is the purpose of this book. If properly understood, however, this concept will enable you to thrive at a Christian college and to understand the purpose of

> *The difference between a Christian university and other institutions of higher education is this: a Christian college weaves a Christian worldview into the entire fabric of the institution, including academic life.*

each class you take, from English literature to organic chemistry. But first we must establish some foundational concepts, the first of which is the notion of a worldview.

What Is a Worldview?

One of the most popular action movies over the past couple of decades was a Keanu Reeves film called *The Matrix*, which spawned— as is typical—several sequels. The film has surprising staying power because amid the fight scenes and big explosions, *The Matrix* forces viewers to ponder the age-old philosophical question posed by Rene Descartes back in the 1600s: How can I know what is really real? The film begins with the protagonist, Neo, as a typical New York City resident. But gradually he becomes enlightened to the true state of reality: computers have taken over the world and are using humans as power supplies, all the while downloading sensory perceptions into their minds to make them think they are living normal modern lives. Neo achieves "salvation" when he accurately perceives the bad guys not as real people but as merely computer-generated programs.

The Matrix thus challenges us to recognize that some of our foundational assumptions about reality—that other people exist, that this laptop I'm writing on is really here—are just that: *assumptions* that serve as starting points for how we perceive our world. If my friend chooses to believe that I am a computer program designed to deceive him, it's unlikely that I can produce evidence that will convince him otherwise. Furthermore, as Neo's experiences in the film indicate, shifting from one perception of reality to another can be a rather jarring, painful process.

In other words, *The Matrix* illustrates this notion of "world-view"—that our prior assumptions about reality shape how we perceive the world around us. A worldview can be defined as a framework of ideas, values, and beliefs about the basic makeup of the world. It is revealed in how we answer basic questions of life, such as: Who am I? Does God exist? Is there a purpose to the universe? Are moral values absolute or relative? What is reality? How should I live my life?

We can think of a worldview as a pair of glasses through which we view our world. We do not so much focus on the lenses; in fact, we often forget they are even there (think again of those two young fish in the opening story). Rather, we look *through* the lenses to view the rest of the world. Or here's another metaphor: if you have ever done a jigsaw puzzle, you know that the picture on the puzzle box is vital. It helps you know where a particular piece fits into the overall puzzle. A worldview does the same. It's the picture on the puzzle box of our lives, by which we make sense of the thousands of experiences that bombard us every day.

Two important qualifications about this notion of "worldview" are important at the outset. First, a worldview is not the same thing as a "life philosophy." A philosophy of life implies a rational, deliberately constructed, formal system of thought that one applies to one's world. But worldviews go deeper than that. A worldview is more *pre* rational and intuitive. It is shaped less by logical analysis than by personal identity (white, black, male, female, young, old, etc.), experiences, and the community in which one lives. I could say that my worldview originates in my *heart* as well as my head. It's the means by which I "know" that 2 + 2 = 4, but it's also how I know that I love my wife, that Jesus is my Savior, and what the appropriate "social space" is in our culture. As Christians, we should, of course, seek to align our worldview with the truth of Scripture and with sound reason (and that's an important purpose of college). But we need to recognize at the outset that a worldview is rooted in who we are at our deepest level, not just our intellect. As C. S. Lewis remarks in *The Magician's Nephew*, "For what you see and hear depends a good deal on where you are standing; it also depends on what sort of person you are."

Second, it's important to note that worldviews are about *actions*, not just beliefs. As one scholar has stated, it is a view *of* the world that governs our behavior *in* the world. To return to the example of Neo in *The Matrix*, his new understanding of the nature of reality results in a fundamental change in how he lives his life. Indeed, one could say that the actions and practices that order our lives reveal what our actual worldview is, regardless of how we might describe that worldview in words. Moreover, because worldviews are lived rather than just pondered, as the philosopher James K. A. Smith observes, the actions that we perform repeatedly can shape who we are, how we think, and even what we believe.

> *All education, whether religious or secular, comes with a built-in point of view.*

We cannot help but have a worldview; like the pair of spectacles perched on my nose, my worldview exists and is constantly interpreting reality for me and guiding my actions, whether I notice it or not. Neo begins *The Matrix* with a worldview; it just happens to be a mistaken one, and he has never bothered to think critically about what his worldview is. One of the main purposes of college, therefore, is to help students recognize, examine, and adjust their worldviews. Which brings me to the second foundational concept.

All Education Comes with a Worldview

Worldviews shape not just our individual lives but institutions, including universities. There was a time when many scholars believed that education was an objective process. Professors in the secular academy, it was claimed, simply "studied the facts" and communicated those facts to their students. Or they forced students to filter their preconceived notions through a supposedly objective scientific grid. Now we know better. All education, whether religious or secular, comes with a built-in point of view. Even in academic disciplines, where critical inquiry is valued, the worldview of the scholar shapes how the information is interpreted and even what information "counts" in the first place. Nothing illustrates this fact better than the following optical illusion commonly used in psychology.

Some viewers immediately see an old lady when they look at this drawing. Others see a young woman. Eventually, just about anyone will be able to see both. (If you cannot, relax and keep looking!) This is because while the actual black and

Fig. 1.1. Old Lady, or Young Woman?

white lines on the page (the "facts," so to speak) remain constant, our minds arrange and interpret these lines in different ways to create a coherent image. Moreover, this isn't something that we consciously decide to do; our minds do it automatically. Finally, it would difficult for those who interpret the drawing in different ways to argue objectively about whose view is the correct one, since their disagreement is not so much over the details of the drawing but over what those "facts" mean.

In a more complex way, a similar process occurs when scholars work in their disciplines. Historians, for example, agree on many events of the American Revolution—that on April 18, 1775, Paul Revere rode through the New England countryside shouting, "The British are coming!"; that the Continental Congress approved the Declaration of Independence on July 4, 1776; that on December 25, 1776, George Washington and his army crossed the Delaware River and surprised Hessian soldiers at Trenton. But what do these facts *mean*? How are they to be arranged into a coherent whole? When did the American Revolution actually begin? What was the prime motivation? Was the victory of the colonists ultimately achieved because of superior tactics, economic factors, French naval support, or something else?

Historians argue constantly over such questions, and the answers to them depend in part on the worldview of the historian, who selects and interprets historical data according to certain assumptions about how societies change—ultimately, basic assumptions about what makes humans tick. Thus, a Marxist historian who believes that ultimately human beings are economic creatures motivated by material rewards will likely interpret the American

Revolution in a way that emphasizes the financial self-interest of colonial elites. The Christian who believes that human motivation often runs deeper than just economic interests will likely include other factors such as ideas and religious impulses. The "facts" of the Revolution are the same for each historian, but like Neo's perception of his world, the *interpretation* of those facts is influenced by the scholar's worldview.

Or, to cite an example from science, biologists generally agree about the makeup of the cell, the structure of DNA, and even the commonality of DNA between humans and other life forms. But do such facts demonstrate that human beings randomly evolved from other life forms, or do they indicate that some sort of intelligent being superintended the process to create humans and other life forms? The answer to this question is not simply a matter of evidence; it is influenced by the scientist's assumptions about ultimate reality.

More generally, not just academic disciplines but entire universities operate according to worldviews. One of the universities that I attended, the University of Michigan, had a worldview that shaped its culture; it was just never stated as such. In fact, one could argue that like many secular universities, my alma mater was animated by a multiplicity of worldviews, not all of which were necessarily coherent. In the classroom, many courses were taught from a perspective known as scientific materialism, which could be described like this: the material universe is all that exists; human beings are a complex life form that evolved randomly over the course of millions of years; belief in God is a trait that evolved relatively recently as a way for humans to explain their origins, but now this belief is no longer necessary. Thus, academic inquiry is best conducted when one sets aside any prior faith commitments.

On the campus quad, however, a different worldview tended to prevail—one of intense scrutiny of words and behaviors based on moral values such as racial justice, gender equality, sexual tolerance, and environmental care. The actions of individuals and the university community, therefore, were rigorously scrutinized according to how they measured up to these moral values, and anyone from the custodian to the president was liable to censure if their words or actions were seen as detrimental to these causes.

Paradoxically, student life at Michigan generally embodied yet another worldview—that of hedonism, or devotion to pleasure. This worldview holds that in the absence of any higher purpose to life, personal pleasure, professional success, and financial security are the greatest values. Thus, one should earn good grades in college since that is the ticket to a successful career. Such studies, however, should not interfere with enjoying college life, especially weekend parties and college football.

The Christian College: A Unified Worldview

From a Christian perspective, one could argue that each of the worldviews I encountered at Michigan contains an element of truth (though we'll wait until Chapter Three to make that argument). Moreover, many Christians—myself included—have excellent experiences at such schools. The problem with the non-Christian university is simply that it's not able to articulate and apply an overarching worldview that gives a coherent purpose to all its parts. As a former college president has remarked, the modern university is not a *uni*versity at all but rather a *multi*versity.

A Christian university, by contrast, operates under an over-arching framework that gives a sense of purpose and unity for everything from English literature to chapel to intramural soccer. That umbrella, of course, is a Christian worldview. Novelist Dorothy Sayers once remarked, "We have rather lost sight of the idea that Christianity is supposed to be an interpretation of the universe." The Christian college proceeds from the assumption that this Christian interpretation of the universe, based in the story of Scripture, affects every aspect of the college experience. The particular elements will be explained in greater detail in the chapters that follow, but briefly, the Christian worldview can be summarized as a grand drama in three main acts.

> *A Christian university . . . operates under an overarching framework that gives a sense of purpose and unity for everything from English literature to chapel to intramural soccer.*

Act 1: Creation. The universe didn't come about by chance. Rather, an all-knowing, all-powerful, triune God created everything that exists. Moreover, God called his creation good and delights in it. God culminated his creative work by making humans in his own image and giving them the capacity to delight in creation and act as "subcreators" themselves.

Act 2: Fall. Human beings, created with a free will, used their freedom to disobey God. All of creation bears the marks of the Fall, from broken human relationships to viruses that kill thousands and wreck economies.

Act 3: Redemption and Consummation. God, however, immediately set about redeeming his fallen creation and restoring it to its original goodness. The key player in the redemptive drama is Jesus Christ, who came to earth as God incarnate to take the penalty for sin upon himself. Eventually history will culminate in the reestablishment of God's reign throughout the entire universe. In the meantime, the followers of Jesus carry out God's redemptive activity in every corner of creation.

That's the biblical narrative in a nutshell, and it has tremendous implications for a Christian college. Plants thrive when they are exposed to a healthy combination of sunlight and rain. Similarly, we can think of creation and redemption as complementary purposes that give life to virtually every aspect of a Christian college.

Here's an example in athletics. A Christian college doesn't just have a college basketball team to boost school spirit or attract attention, as secular colleges typically do. Rather, basketball fulfills both a creative and a redemptive purpose for Christians. God delights in his creation, and he created human beings in his image to delight in creation as well. Thus, human play honors God, and developing our ability to shoot a basketball—or spike a volleyball, or swing a golf club—is a way to more fully express God's image.

College sports, however, also bear the marks of the fall. Athletes are placed on pedestals, coaches sometimes cheat, and heated contests can degenerate into hatred toward referees and opposing players. A Christian college, therefore, also plays basketball in order to "redeem" this particular corner of God's creation by fielding teams that demonstrate sportsmanship and fans who act generously toward opponents and even to referees (that's the ideal, at least).

Beyond the extracurricular, the Christian worldview provides a sense of purpose in the classroom as well as on the court. This concept will be explored in detail in subsequent chapters, but for now let me illustrate with an example from a common major—business. One thing that we learn in the book of Genesis is that God intended for humans to live and function together in community. That's why he created Adam and Eve. He also designed his creation to increase in complexity and interdependence. Today we see that complexity in virtually every aspect of life. Take, for example, my morning cup of coffee, which would be impossible if I were left to my own resources. The beans for my coffee are grown and harvested on a hillside in Colombia. They are transported to my local grocery store, where I buy a pound of them for a few dollars. The parts for my coffee maker are produced and assembled elsewhere, and the electricity that makes it work is generated by a plant that converts the water flowing from the nearby Grand River into usable power. Simply put, my cup of coffee represents the tip of an iceberg of complex human interactions. And that's a good thing; it's how the world was intended to function.

In its most basic sense, the academic discipline of business is about learning how to efficiently and justly manage the countless economic and social transactions that we depend on each day. In other words, it's about developing our capacity to live out the notion of human interdependence that was part of God's original design for his creation.

The study of business, however, also has a redemptive component. Unfortunately, economic relations are corrupted by all sorts of individual and structural sin. We see this most obviously, of course, in the corporate scandals that periodically make the headlines. But the effects of the Fall also exist under the radar in economic injustices that might be unwittingly perpetuated even by the coffee beans that I purchase. How does one create a business that pays coffee growers in Colombia a fair price for their beans and still turns a profit in the United States? How do communities produce the power needed for their coffeemakers while also caring for the environment? How does one responsibly generate wealth and the opportunity to enable others to benefit from good-paying jobs? These are the sorts of questions that courses in business must deal with at a Christian college. In other words, Christians don't just study business in order to make money; they explore how best to practice human interdependence and to redeem economic relations that have been damaged and distorted by the Fall.

In sum, everything you do at a Christian college has a purpose and value within a Christian framework. Determining what that purpose is, however, isn't always easy, since as the final section explains, worldviews don't stay the same.

Worldviews Are Dynamic and Open-Ended

Far from being static, our worldviews change and develop as we encounter new people, ideas, and experiences. Thus, the purpose of a Christian college isn't simply to hand you a complete Christian worldview on a platter. Rather, it's to start you on the *process* of developing a comprehensive, coherent, yet flexible Christian worldview. This doesn't mean that we hold Christianity as a tentative hypothesis that we're ready to drop if some new idea comes along. But it does mean that we hold many of our beliefs loosely and remain open to adjusting our Christian worldview as we encounter new ideas and experiences in college.

Let me illustrate it this way: I love crossword puzzles. Back in high school, they got me through more than a few dull classes (and probably lowered my GPA as well). Crossword puzzles can help us understand how knowledge and beliefs actually work. That's because, often, the correct answer to a particular crossword clue is initially uncertain. Its "truth" must be supported by other clues in the puzzle. The key to solving a crossword puzzle is to build a network of interlocking answers that support each other and form a coherent whole. A completed

> *The purpose of a Christian college isn't simply to hand you a complete Christian worldview on a platter. Rather, it's to start you on the process of developing a comprehensive, coherent, yet flexible Christian worldview.*

crossword puzzle, therefore, is constructed painstakingly through a back-and-forth process of trial and error. Here's a simple example:

Across

1. A freshwater fish

Down

2. The top of an arc

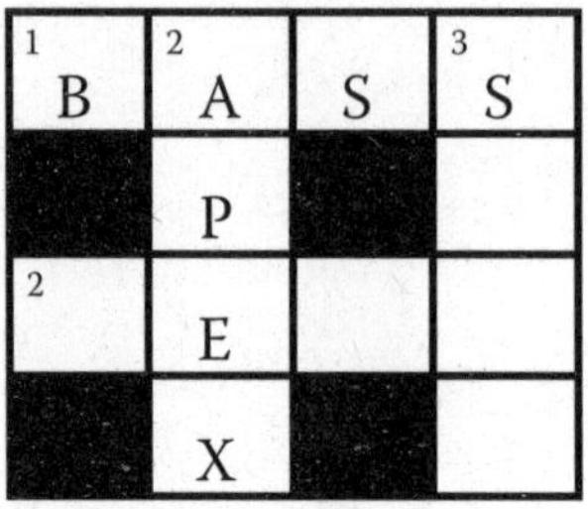

¹B	²A	S	³S
■	P	■	
²	E	■	
■	X	■	

Fig. 1.2.

If these were the only questions that you had to answer, the solutions might seem simple: "BASS" and "APEX" seem to fit nicely. But let's add two more clues:

Across

1. A freshwater fish
2. Look intently

Down

2. The top of an arc
3. Meat from a pig

The word "PEER" seems to work fine for "Look intently." But after trying and failing to think of "meat from a pig" that begins with an *S*, you would probably conclude that "PORK" is the only possible answer to 3 Down. But what about "BASS"? You need to go back and erase the word, change it to "CARP," and the puzzle is solved. How do you know your solution is true? Because the answers fit together and support each other.

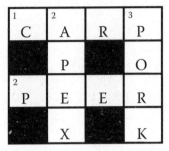

Fig. 1.3.

So what does this have to do with a Christian worldview? Plenty. We can think of our particular beliefs as answers to individual clues and a worldview as the entire crossword puzzle formed by these interlocking, mutually supporting beliefs. Experienced puzzlers use pencil, not pen, to do crosswords since they know that successfully solving the puzzle inevitably involves going back and erasing some earlier answers in light of later information. Of course, some answers are so clearly correct that they can be written in pen. If I get this clue, for example—"Former Chicago Bulls great Michael" (six letters)—I can confidently write "JORDAN" in permanent ink. The key is to recognize which answers are certain and which ones are up for debate.

Obviously, some components of our Christian worldview can be written in pen. For example, if we have a five-letter box and the clue is "the Son of God," we can safely write "Jesus" in pen. However, Christians have often tended to use too much pen when formulating their worldview. For example, Christians in the Middle Ages generally believed that the earth was the center of the universe around which the sun and planets revolved. When Galileo proposed otherwise, he was placed under house arrest. Why? Because the church interpreted verses such as Psalm 104:5 ("He set the earth on its foundations; it can never be moved") to teach that the earth is fixed at the center of the universe, and the sun and planets revolve around it. Today, of course, we see such an interpretation as a result of mistaken medieval cosmology, not as a necessary teaching of Scripture. Medieval Christians, however, had penned in as an absolute truth the notion that the earth is at the center of creation, when they should have used pencil.

Students often arrive at college with much of their worldview written in pen. In fact, many of us come from churches, schools, or communities that encourage us to fill in the puzzle with as much pen as possible. On the other hand, we also inhabit a society—the culture of "you do you"—that disbelieves in any absolute truths and enshrines personal freedom as the only universal principle worth holding. The combination of these influences can leave us feeling scattered, perhaps even schizophrenic, intellectually and spiritually. That's why a key purpose of a Christian college is to help you learn to balance the pen and the pencil, if you will, to develop a healthy balance of convictions that are open to revision and those that are not. Solving a crossword puzzle is more of an art than a science, and so is developing a firm but flexible Christian faith.

Worldviews Are Formed in Community

Finally, the crossword puzzle analogy also helps explain the value of a diverse community to Christian learning. Any crossword puzzle that is challenging enough to be interesting is also difficult to solve on your own. Once, for example, I was stuck on a seemingly simple section. The four-letter clue was "Jubal's instrument," and knowing from previous clues that the first letter was *L* and the last letter was *E*, I had penciled in "LUTE." Unfortunately, the rest of the puzzle didn't fit. Eventually I gave up and handed the puzzle to my wife, a professional musician, who quickly changed "LUTE" to "LYRE." After that, the rest of the puzzle fell neatly into place.

Similarly, at a Christian university, it's through our encounters with others that we come to notice our unquestioned assumptions, consider new ideas, and hopefully see the world through others' eyes. Not only professors but coaches, residence hall directors, and fellow students bring different perspectives and areas of expertise that help us adjust and perhaps redefine our own worldviews. Some of my most formative learning experiences in Bible college were late-night conversations in the dormitory with students from Indonesia, Kenya, and Honduras who exposed me to fascinating new ways of seeing the world. My faith developed in ways that would have been impossible apart from Christian community.

Of course, all analogies are imperfect, and the crossword puzzle metaphor falls short in two important ways. First, solving a crossword puzzle has never, to my recollection, changed the way I live. A worldview, however, is intimately connected to and shaped by behavior. That's why the Christian college ultimately seeks to produce graduates who not only apply a Christian worldview to their academic disciplines but who *live* their lives differently. As one educator has stated, a Christian college is a workshop in meaningful, intentional Christian living. Discipleship, not intellectual analysis, is the goal of a Christian education.

Second, when I complete a crossword puzzle, I wad it up and throw it away. A worldview, however, is never fully complete. One doesn't spend four years of college constructing a worldview, then place it on the shelf and walk away. A Christian worldview helps us make sense of our lives and gives a sense of purpose to everything we do, both individually and collectively. But just as Galileo's discoveries necessitated a change to the medieval worldview, so new insights and experiences require that we reexamine and adjust our Christian worldview throughout our lives, and alter our way of life accordingly. In other words, both the pen and the pencil are parts of the mature Christian's tool kit, and the college years are a good time to learn to use them.

> *Why does college matter? Because it prepares us to be image bearers of God and effective agents of redemption in every corner of creation.*

Like the two younger fish in David Foster Wallace's commencement address, it's easy to swim through the "water" of American culture, including college, without ever questioning what it is we're actually doing, or why. Making the most of college, however, begins with asking why you're investing significant time and effort in higher education, and that "why" question should extend to every course that you take. Why does college matter? Because it prepares us to be image bearers of God and effective agents of redemption in every corner of creation. This book will unpack and explain that notion more fully—but we'll begin with a brief look at where the notion of a Christian college came from in the first place.

A Note on Sources

The literature on Christian worldview and education is vast. Two standard older texts are Richard Middleton and Brian Walsh, *The Transforming Vision: Shaping a Christian Worldview* (Downers Grove, IL: InterVarsity Press, 1984), and James Sire, *The Universe Next Door* (Downers Grove, IL: InterVarsity Press, 1974). Recent works include David Naugle, *Worldview: The History of a Concept* (Grand Rapids: Eerdmans, 2002), and Albert Wolters, *Creation Regained* (Grand Rapids: Eerdmans, 2005). More recently, James K. A. Smith has sought to ground the notion of worldview in the affections and in liturgical practice in *Desiring the Kingdom: Worship, Worldview, and Cultural Formation* (Ada, MI: Baker Academic, 2009).

David Foster Wallace's 2005 Kenyon College commencement address can be found on several sites online, including the Farnam Street website: https://fs.blog/2012/04/david-foster-wallace-this-is-water/. The observation that "worldview" involves knowing from the heart as well as the mind is found in George Pierson, "Evangelicals and Worldview Confusion," in *After Worldview: Christian Higher Education in Postmodern Worlds*, ed. Matt Bonzo and Michael Stevens (Sioux Center, IA: Dordt College Press, 2009). The quotations from C. S. Lewis, *The Magician's Nephew* and from Dorothy Sayers are from David Naugle, "Worldview: History, Theology, Implications," in *After Worldview*, ed. Bonzo and Stevens, 26 and 6.

Questions for Reflection and Discussion

1. What worldviews have you encountered so far in your educational background? What actions revealed them?

2. What have been the main influences in your life so far in shaping your own worldview? What examples demonstrate their influence on you?

3. Other than professors, who do you anticipate having the most impact on your worldview during your college years? Why?

4. What beliefs that you have brought with you to college are written in "pen"? What beliefs are written in "pencil"?

5. How should we determine which of our beliefs are open to revision and which ones are not?

2 WHERE WE CAME FROM

A History of Christian Colleges in America

I met my wife in college—in the first week, to be exact. After we met, some of the first questions we asked each other were, Where are you from? and What is your family like? That's because, as everyone instinctively knows, one of the best ways to understand a person is to become familiar with his or her past.

The same principle applies to institutions. Anyone planning to spend their next four or five years at a Christian college should have some awareness of where these institutions came from and how they have been shaped over the past few hundred years. In the previous chapter, I briefly discussed the typical worldviews found at the University of Michigan, such as scientific materialism and modern hedonism. It may be surprising, therefore, to learn that in the late 1800s, Michigan was in many ways a thoroughly Christian institution. All of the university's professors affirmed the Christian faith, and President Henry Tappan delivered annual lectures entitled "Evidences of the Christian Religion." Students attended chapel every day and church twice on Sunday.

Michigan wasn't alone in American higher education. Harvard University's original motto, for example, was *Christo et Ecclesiae*— "for Christ and the Church." So what changed, and why? This chapter will explain the Christian vision behind American colleges, how that vision waned in the 1800s, and how today's Christian colleges attempt to forge a distinctively Christian approach to higher education. Of course, this narrative does not characterize in detail every institution of Christian higher education in the United States. In particular, it leaves out Catholic universities, which were isolated from the cultural mainstream for much of American history and were nurtured by theological traditions that far predated America's origins. Nevertheless, the notion that Christian academic institutions are engaged in something of a recovery project—in rebuilding a robust, academically rigorous enterprise of higher education that makes a difference in the world—does describe many Christian colleges today.

Part One:
The Founding and Growth of Christian Colleges, 1600–1860

The story begins four hundred years ago. Among North America's first European settlers was a group of fervent Christians from England known as Puritans. When the main group of Puritans landed in New England in 1630, they immediately set about building shelter, planting crops, and doing other tasks necessary to survive in the North American wilderness. Not long after that—in 1636, to be exact—they founded Harvard College.

The Puritan movement was imbued with a fire for Christian thinking, and so founding a college in the harsh New England wilderness was second nature to them. Harvard College's primary purpose was to train pastors for the Puritan churches, but the college also educated New England's political and social leaders. As for coursework, the college placed a heavy emphasis on Latin, Greek, and Hebrew. It also stressed rhetoric, and to a lesser extent theology, ethics, politics, mathematics, and history. Bible instruction took place on Sunday, when Harvard students had to sit through two lengthy sermons and then repeat them to their tutors on Sunday evening.

Fig. 2.1. Harvard College, 1740

For much of the 1600s, Harvard was the only institution in colonial higher education. In the next century, however, several new Christian colleges were established in the Harvard mold. In 1701, Connecticut Puritans, fearing that Harvard was departing from its Christian moorings, established Yale College. A few decades later, other denominations followed suit. Thus were born many of

America's Ivy League universities as we know them today—schools such as Princeton, Brown, and Dartmouth. Indeed, virtually without exception, American colleges begun in the colonial era were created by Protestants with the explicit purpose of training Christians to effectively engage their culture as leaders in the church and society.

> *Virtually without exception, American colleges begun in the colonial era were created by Protestants with the explicit purpose of training Christians to effectively engage their culture as leaders in the church and society.*

This isn't to say that Christian education in the 1700s was a Golden Age, by any means. In the classroom, professors typically employed the less-than-inspiring "recitation" method: students memorized the lecture for the day and then regurgitated it back to a tutor. Some students, forced to attend college by socially ambitious parents, livened up the dull routine by breaking rules, threatening professors, and rioting on occasion.

However, for all of their short-comings, Puritan colleges embodied an ideal that will be explored in further detail in subsequent chapters—that Christian thinking should embrace not just the Bible but should range over *all* subjects; that as God's image bearers we are called to pursue truth in all areas. Twentieth-century educator Henry Zylstra put it in words the Puritan founders would affirm: "In Christian education, nothing matters but the kingdom of Jesus Christ; but because of the kingdom, everything else matters." The Puritans made no distinction between Christian and secular subjects—it was all God's world out there for his creatures to explore and enjoy.

The Old-Time College

American Christians took a break from college building in the late 1700s as the American Revolution took center stage. In the 1800s, however, a host of new colleges arrived on the scene. Some of these—Catholic universities—were an entirely new type, at least from the perspective of American Protestants. Roman Catholic immigrants did not arrive in the United States in large numbers until the late 1700s. Excluded from mainstream society, they quickly began building their own educational institutions, beginning with Georgetown University in 1791. Other Catholic colleges soon followed, including one, Notre Dame, that gladly adopted as its mascot the Protestants' stereotype of Catholic immigrants: the "Fighting Irish."

Protestants as well as Catholics engaged in college building in the 1800s. Spurred on by a series of religious revivals known as the Second Great Awakening, they founded Christian colleges by the hundreds—over five hundred of them, to be exact, though only about two hundred survived into the twentieth century. For countless communities, establishing a Christian college was not so much a response to overwhelming demand for education as it was a way to assert a town's significance and community spirit. These schools came to be known as "Old-Time Colleges," and they had several features in common.

Fig. 2.2. Old Brick Row, Yale College, 1807

First, Old-Time Colleges exuded a strongly Christian ethos. College presidents were typically Christian ministers, and professors were expected to be generalists who could teach just about everything. The goal of the college curriculum was not so much to impart particular knowledge as to develop a mature, balanced Christian young person who thought clearly and behaved morally. This was best done, it was believed, through a balanced assortment of courses in literature, science, and the arts.

Concerning student life, the colleges operated *in loco parentis*—"in the place of parents"—and strictly regulated the lives of students. Colleges specified times for waking up, studying, attending classes, playing, and retiring. A host of rules governed student life; "amusements" such as Sabbath breaking, card playing, alcohol, tobacco, foul language, and disorderly conduct were prohibited. Students attended chapel daily and church twice on Sunday. As one might imagine, such strict supervision could at times spark resistance, and student riots were not uncommon. Princeton College, for example, experienced six separate riots between 1800 and 1830, one of which left the campus's main building, Nassau Hall, in ashes.

As an antidote to student rebellion, colleges promoted revivals to heighten the religious fervor of the student body. Yale College was especially known for the intensity of its campus revivals. Throughout the 1800s, Yale stood as the premier Christian college in the nation both in its academic quality and in the spiritual fervor of its students. Its graduates fanned out across the South and West, founding and presiding over new Christian colleges, thus earning Yale the reputation as the nineteenth century's "mother of colleges." Such religious characteristics were not limited to private colleges. As mentioned earlier, even most public universities of the day saw themselves as essentially Christian institutions.

In all, the colleges and universities in the mid-1800s, on the eve of the Civil War, reflected the beliefs and values of America's most dominant cultural group, white middle-class Protestants. Little did they realize that in a few decades, American university life would be almost completely secular and Christian colleges would be relegated to the cultural backwaters of society.

Part Two
The Collapse and Revival of the Christian College, 1860–2020

To understand the swift collapse of Old-Time Colleges in the late nineteenth century, we must explore these institutions more deeply. American Christian higher education in the 1800s seemed quite healthy, but this outward strength masked serious internal weaknesses. First, these institutions were essentially havens for a small group of privileged white males. Except for innovative Oberlin College and a few other institutions, women and African Americans were largely excluded from nineteenth-century colleges. In 1870, only 1.7 percent of American young people aged 18 to 21 were enrolled in colleges and universities. The diversity of students that has come to characterize many Christian colleges today was almost entirely absent in the 1800s. College was essentially a four-year rite of passage for members of the nation's privileged class before they took their positions in ministry, law, or medicine.

For anyone else in nineteenth-century America, college was largely perceived as impractical and irrelevant. The colleges maintained a rigid classical curriculum in which all students took the same classes throughout their four years of study. The system neglected the educational interests of some of the most productive members of society, such as farmers, businessmen, and mechanics. As a result, many colleges went extinct, and those that survived were forced to keep student costs artificially low in order to maintain enrollment. College professors often bore the brunt of the colleges' financial problems, earning paltry salaries that barely kept them above the poverty level. Not that such professors were likely to earn higher pay elsewhere. Typically kindly old gentlemen, college professors hardly commanded respect as an intellectual force in society. Remarked the nineteenth-century Bostonian Henry Adams about the professors in his day: "No one took Harvard College seriously."

Adams's remark points to the most serious weakness of the nineteenth-century Christian college: its lack of deep, intentional, rigorous Christian thinking across a range of subjects that had characterized the Puritans. As historian Mark Noll has noted, because

Protestant educators' values fit so neatly with that of the surrounding society, they neglected to develop a clear Christian foundation for or critique of their cultural situation. They failed, in Noll's words, "to push thinking from the Scripture to modern situations and back again." For example, in a society in which the enslavement of black people was considered by most Americans to be acceptable, most Christian colleges failed to ask deep questions about how social norms did or did not reflect the will of God.

> *Because Protestant educators' values fit so neatly with that of the surrounding society, they neglected to develop a clear Christian foundation for or critique of their cultural situation.*

In all, Protestants created colleges that promoted warmhearted evangelical spirituality and the formation of moral character, but that generally failed to offer a well-rounded Christian approach to higher education. When dramatic changes hit American society in the late 1800s, the Old-Time Colleges discovered that they had been built on shifting sand.

The Secularization of the University

The first major development to affect Christian colleges was a change in the nature of science. Nineteenth-century Christians had believed that doing science was simply a matter of organizing one's observations of the natural world into general laws that revealed God's goodness and purpose in creation—that, in other words, science always confirmed the Bible. By the mid-1800s, however, new views of science emerging in Europe challenged this notion. Scientists, European scholars asserted, should be guided by the assumption that all phenomena originated from *natural*, not supernatural, causes. The task of the scientist, therefore, was to trace events to their natural causes, thereby excluding any considerations of God's design and activity in creation.

Charles Darwin's theory of evolution, which was publicized in 1859, was both a product of and a catalyst for this new intellectual trend. Darwin argued that humans were not created by God but rather evolved through random changes over millions of years. Such a theory seemed to contradict Christians' belief in the literal truth of Genesis as well as the comforting notion that science revealed evidence of God's handiwork in nature. Christians who had assured themselves that science invariably supported Christian faith could offer little by way of effective response now that science seemed to point in the opposite direction.

Fig. 2.3. The Cornell University Library, 1891

At the same time scientists were questioning Christian intellectual foundations, vast new financial sources for modern universities emerged that dwarfed the budgets of the Old-Time Colleges. In 1862, Congress passed the Morrill Act, which made government funds available for states to establish public universities, such as Michigan State and Texas A&M, that would advance practical education in the areas of agriculture and mechanics. Government support for higher education was joined by private donations. The industrial society of the late 1800s produced fabulously wealthy men such as Ezra Cornell, Johns Hopkins, and Cornelius Vanderbilt. These industrialists poured huge sums of money into universities bearing their names, both as a means of boosting their own stature and to generate the scientific discoveries and technological know-how needed by the new industrial society.

Thus was born the public research university that has become a fixture in modern America, and which vastly overshadowed the pre–Civil War Christian college in size, money, and social prominence. Where the Old-Time College counted its students in the hundreds, the new universities educated thousands. In 1850, for example, about 28,000 Americans were enrolled in college—far fewer than the 72,000 spectators who filled Michigan Stadium, built in the early 1900s, to watch the Wolverines play college football on a Saturday afternoon. In 1824, Princeton College was considered audacious when it sought to raise $100,000 from its alumni. A half-century later, Johns Hopkins, a banker and investor in the Baltimore & Ohio Railroad, personally donated $3.5 million to establish a German-style research university.

Rather than hiring retired ministers to teach everything from geometry to ancient history, the modern university employed trained experts in particular fields. The PhD, not personal piety, became the most desirable quality in professors. The new universities changed what students studied as well. In 1870, Harvard president Charles Eliot discarded the college's traditional classical curriculum and introduced the elective system, whereby students chose their own course of study from a number of different subjects and departments. Eliot's innovation proved so successful in attracting students that other universities soon followed suit. By the end of the century the classical curriculum was rapidly disappearing in American higher education.

Amid the specialized departments of the modern university, however, the attempt to understand and present a unified body of knowledge about the world largely disappeared.

Like most big changes that occur in history, the rise of the secular research university was neither all good nor all bad. Clearly, the new universities brought about academic and social improvements. They expressed a basic Christian principle that education should affect the way we live and bring about positive changes in society. Amid the specialized departments of the modern university, however, the attempt to understand and present a unified body of knowledge about the world largely disappeared. Moreover, the traditional Christian college's commitment to forming the character of its students—for linking the head and the heart—gradually evaporated. The modern university was a secular enterprise designed to produce competency in a professional and technological society; Christian perspectives that got in the way of progress and impeded scientific advancement were excluded outright or pushed to the margins of university life.

So how did Christians in higher education respond to these new developments? Generally in two ways, neither of which were adequate. First, many Christian colleges sought to keep up with the new trends by abandoning or obscuring their religious identity. Rather than discarding Christian belief immediately, such colleges typically redefined Christianity as devotion to high moral ideals or service to humanity. Eventually, even the Christian rhetoric disappeared as these institutions became smaller versions of the secular research university. Thus, on many campuses today, chapel buildings and campus inscriptions such as Harvard's *Christo et Ecclesiae* function largely as vestiges of a bygone era in American higher education.

Fig. 2.4. The Harvard Seal, 1700   The Harvard Seal, 1900

Of course, not all Americans abandoned Christian higher education in the late 1800s. Catholic universities remained largely unaffected by the secularizing tendencies of the day. Furthermore, many Protestant colleges with close connections to denominations such as Baptist, Lutheran, Presbyterian, and Mennonite sustained a commitment to Christian higher education. But within the mainstream Protestant colleges, especially those without strong denominational ties, a more defensive, anti-intellectual posture tended to take root. Conservative evangelical Christians at the turn of the century feared that American culture was slipping from its Christian foundations, and that included the nation's colleges. "Christian schools were once the pride of our nation," declared pastor T. C. Horton. "Now, many are the progeny of Satan." Thus, conservatives transformed existing institutions such as Wheaton College in Illinois and created "Bible colleges" like the Bible Institute of Los Angeles (BIOLA) to provide a Christian education that they believed was disappearing in the culture at large.

These "evangelical" colleges admirably strove to provide a semblance of Christian education in a secularizing age. However, as well-rounded Christian intellectual institutions, they displayed serious shortcomings. Bible colleges sought to provide brief, practical training for young people who planned to become full-time Christian workers. This emphasis on "practical" Christian education led such institutions to neglect an interest in a wide range of subjects and academic disciplines. As historian Virginia Brereton has observed, "General education was considered an unwanted extravagance given the exigencies of the time." The Bible college's focus on evangelism and missions tended to crowd out a healthy interest in all God's creation that the Puritan colleges had displayed.

Furthermore, many conservative Christians in the early twentieth century developed a preoccupation with end-of-the-world biblical prophecy—especially the belief in an imminent "rapture" of believers to heaven—which led them to de-emphasize attention to the affairs of the visible world. Why study politics or biology, they reasoned, if the world is about to end soon anyway? Secular learning came to be seen either as a set of false ideas to be refuted or as dangerous to the faith of Christian young people and thus best left alone. Subjects such as Bible, apologetics, and evangelism seemed safer and more practical.

In all, Christian colleges tended to exchange one overly simplistic approach to American culture with another: while Christian colleges in the 1800s tended to assume they had a privileged role of *dominance* in American culture, the evangelical colleges of the early 1900s generally sought *separation* from their surrounding culture. Thus, while Christian higher education in the twentieth century continued in the wake of secularization, in many cases it was only a shadow of the robust vision articulated by earlier Christians.

Reviving Christian Higher Education

In the past half century, however, Christian colleges have grown in size, quality, and awareness of their cultural task. Part of their revival is due to the growth of American conservative Christianity in general. While liberal Protestantism has declined in recent decades, evangelical churches have generally increased in size and resources. Thus, there are more students available to populate evangelical Christian colleges, and financially successful Christians have more money to invest in them. In 1976, thirty-eight intentionally

Christ-centered colleges in the United States joined together to form the Council for Christian Colleges & Universities (CCCU). The organization now has over 180 members and affiliates worldwide that collectively enroll over five hundred thousand students. CCCU schools in the United States experienced 18 percent growth in full-time enrollment from 2003 to 2015, well above the national average.

As they increased in size, Christian colleges also witnessed a revival of interest in breadth of learning in all disciplines. The catalyst for this recovery was Abraham Kuyper, a nineteenth-century Dutch Reformed theologian and politician. Kuyper urged Christians of his day to engage their culture, and he articulated an approach to learning in which Christian truths were integrated into all academic disciplines. As Kuyper put it, "There is not a square inch on the whole plain of human existence over which Christ, who is Lord over all, does not proclaim, 'This is Mine!'" In Kuyper's philosophy, chemistry, psychology, history, and sociology had as much place in the Christian college curriculum as theology and philosophy. Moreover, Kuyper sought to *integrate* Christian faith with learning in every discipline.

Kuyper's educational approach impacted Calvin College, a Christian Reformed school in Michigan, in the mid-twentieth century. Later, when several colleges joined with Calvin to form the Christian College Coalition, Kuyper's influence spread throughout American Christian higher education. Eventually, it impacted even major universities such as Notre Dame and Baylor, when former Calvin College professors nurtured in Kuyper's worldview assumed influential faculty positions at those institutions. By the 1980s, the "integration" model of faith and learning, which we will explore in Chapter Six, had come to permeate many Christian colleges, prompting them to promote a distinctively Christian approach to learning.

The Christian college in America today represents something different than simply a return to the Old-Time College of the 1800s. For example, the nineteenth-century model of the professor as a kindly old "jack of all trades" may have encouraged the development of Christian character, but it did not always challenge students to love God with their minds. Generally speaking, Christian college professors today are both mentors who care about the spiritual development of students *and* competent scholars in their academic disciplines. One important lesson of the past two centuries is that it was not too much thinking that led colleges to secularize; rather, it was a *lack* of clear, rigorous Christian thinking applied to the wide range of emerging academic disciplines that led institutions to see Christianity as basically irrelevant to their mission. Christian professors who combine spiritual commitment and academic excellence make secularization less likely.

> *By the 1980s, the "integration" model of faith and learning . . . had come to permeate many Christian colleges, prompting them to promote a distinctively Christian approach to learning.*

Second, the lengthy lists of rules and restrictions on students' lives that characterized nineteenth-century colleges have grown shorter over the years. Christian educators today do not see their role as primarily *in loco parentis*, but rather as helping form students into mature Christians who demonstrate wisdom and own their faith for themselves. Christian colleges now generally seek a greater balance between community standards and personal freedom in their lifestyle expectations.

Fig. 2.5. Cathedral of the Ozarks on the campus of John Brown University

Third, modern Christian colleges display a broader course of study than those of the past. The nineteenth-century college curriculum rooted in the classics, while valuable, made no allowance for a student's unique intellectual interests and career goals. Christian colleges today recognize that part of their mission is equipping students to effectively engage their culture as Christians in their professions. Thus, they typically combine required classes in the Christian liberal arts with more professionally oriented studies in a major of one's choice.

Finally, in a society still marked by racial injustice, Christian colleges in the twenty-first century have developed a stronger commitment to issues of diversity and inclusion on campus. For example, staff positions focused on issues of campus diversity have been established at many Christian college campuses, and since 2016 the Council for Christian Colleges & Universities has hosted an annual Diversity Conference. In terms of demographics, Christian colleges have begun to more accurately reflect the diverse society of both the United States and the Christian church. In 1999, over 80 percent of students who attended CCCU schools were white. By 2018, the percentage of nonwhite students at CCCU schools had nearly doubled, from 20 percent to 40 percent, and that number continues to increase each year. While changes to the makeup of faculty and administration are proceeding more slowly, progress continues to be made in that area as well. Between 2008 and 2018, for example, the number of faculty of color in the CCCU doubled from 10 percent to 20 percent.

Christian colleges are by no means perfect. Since the 2009 recession, some have struggled to enroll enough students to maintain healthy budgets. Moreover, faculty and student accomplishments at secular universities—not to mention financial resources—often exceed those of Christian colleges. Nevertheless, these colleges have managed to maintain a commitment to distinctively Christian education, even when that vision was challenged by the broader society and when many leading institutions abandoned such a vision. The next few chapters will explore how the basic elements of the Christian story can make a profound difference to Christian learning.

A Note on Sources

There are a number of excellent historical works that detail the history of American Christian colleges and American Christian thinking in general. Among the best are George Marsden, *The Soul of the American University* (Oxford: Oxford University Press, 1994); William Ringenberg, *The Christian College* (Grand Rapids: Eerdmans, 2006); James Burtchaell, *The Dying of the Light* (Grand Rapids: Eerdmans, 1998); Joel Carpenter and Kenneth Shipps, *Making Higher Education Christian* (Grand Rapids: Eerdmans, 1987); Richard Hughes and William Adrian, *Models for Christian Higher Education* (Grand Rapids: Eerdmans, 1997); and Mark Noll, *The Scandal of the Evangelical Mind* (Grand Rapids: Eerdmans, 1994). A good comprehensive history of US higher education is John Thelin, *A History of American Higher Education* (Baltimore: Johns Hopkins University Press, 2011).

Henry Zylstra is quoted in Henry Beversluis, "Toward a Theology of Education" (Calvin College Papers, February, 1981), 10. A discussion of student riots is found in Frederick Rudolph, *The American College and University: A History*, 2nd ed. (Athens: University of Georgia Press, 1991), 96–99. Statistics concerning nineteenth-century higher education are drawn from Rudolph, 486, and the 1854 United States Census. Henry Adams's quote comes from Mark Noll's introduction to Ringenberg, *Christian College*, 17. Noll's discussion of the weaknesses in nineteenth-century Christian thought is found in his book *The Scandal of the Evangelical Mind*, 107. T. C. Horton is quoted in the *Ozark American*, September, 1922, 11. Brereton's remark is found in Virginia Brereton, *Training God's Army: The American Bible School, 1880–1940* (Bloomington: Indiana University Press, 1990), 115. Kuyper's statement is quoted in James Bratt and Ronald Wells, "Piety and Progress: A History of Calvin College," in Hughes and Adrian, eds., *Models for Christian Higher Education*, 143. Data about Christian college diversity has been drawn from "Christian Higher Education Becoming Less White," *The Christian Post* (March 4, 2018), and "Diversity within the CCCU," *CCCU Advance* (Spring 2020).

Questions for Reflection and Discussion

1. Do you think that the process of Christian colleges "going secular" is inevitable? Why or why not?

2. What features of Christian colleges of the past are worth emulating today? Which ones are not?

3. What could the colleges of the 1800s have done to avoid becoming secularized?

4. Can Christian colleges de-emphasize rules and still be distinctively Christian? If so, how?

5. What do you think is the value of a network of Christian colleges that is broader than any single institution?

PART TWO

The Christian Story and Christian Learning

3   LIVING LARGELY

The Doctrine of Creation

A couple of years ago, I was driving down a highway near my home in Grand Rapids, Michigan, and I saw a billboard advertisement for a local public university. It depicted a smiling recent graduate under a phrase in large bold letters: "Hire Education." The message was clear: come to our university, and you'll get a good job when you're done.

That sales pitch is not unique. Since World War II, a college education in America has been understood primarily as a means to social and economic mobility. As professors William Willimon and Thomas Naylor chronicled in their 1995 book, *The Abandoned Generation*, the purpose of higher education has been to help students realize their economic potential, or put more crassly, "to become a money-making machine." If anything, that understanding of higher education has become more prevalent over the past two decades. As Jean Twenge documents in her book *iGen*, today's young people are highly concerned with safety and security, and they tend to view a college education as a way to ensure a life of financial security, if not necessarily career fulfillment.

This kind of thinking is not completely off the mark. Christians certainly would agree that there is value in emphasizing career development. The Protestant Reformers of the 1500s criticized what they saw as the world-denying ethic of Roman Catholicism and believed that Christians should value secular occupations. And one of the weaknesses of nineteenth-century colleges was their refusal to develop programs of education that would train the hands of students as well as educating their heads. Hence, at Christian colleges today, admissions counselors, career development officers, and student development professionals promote the economic value of a college education, and the college's job placement rate has become a standard metric of quality.

Nevertheless, Christian colleges stand in opposition to modern culture's understanding of college in some important ways. First, Christians do not believe that one must go to college in order to experience a fulfilled life. A fascinating book by a non-Christian author, Matthew Crawford, entitled *Shop Class as Soulcraft*, makes this point well. Crawford completed a PhD in political philosophy from the University of Chicago and went on to direct a think tank. He then resigned his position to start, of all things, a motorcycle repair shop, where he claimed to find more intellectual challenge and emotional satisfaction in repairing engines than he had in discussing ideas. Crawford's point is one that Christians, who believe that all human labor is noble, can endorse: humans are made for excellence, and they can

> *For Christians, learning is an intrinsic good; education is valuable for its own sake, not just for what you do with it.*

fulfill that calling in a variety of tasks, some of which require a college education and some of which do not. College isn't for everyone, and a college degree should not be used to measure whether one is successful or not.

Second, while in general Christian colleges prepare students for successful careers, they also do much more than that. Christian colleges are founded on the notion that education isn't simply a commodity to be purchased. Rather, for Christians, learning is an *intrinsic* good; education is valuable for its own sake, not just for what you do with it.

To unpack that idea, we need to go back to the Christian creation story as recorded in Genesis 1:

> Then God said, "Let us make mankind in our image, in our likeness, so that they may rule over the fish in the sea and the birds in the sky, over the livestock and all the wild animals, and over all the creatures that move along the ground." So God created mankind in his own image, in the image of God he created them; male and female he created them. God blessed them and said to them, "Be fruitful and increase in number; fill the earth and subdue it. Rule over the fish in the sea and the birds in the sky and over every living creature that moves on the ground." . . . God saw all that he had made, and it was very good. (Gen. 1:26–31)

Christians have often debated how to interpret the early chapters of Genesis. Were the "days" of creation literal twenty-four-hour days? Did God create every species individually, or did some species evolve from others under God's sovereign guidance? During your college years, you will likely have ample opportunity to discuss such questions. But for now, our purpose is to understand the central message of this creation story and how it applies to our lives at a Christian college. In sum, the biblical creation account has four key implications for education.

We Know God Better by Studying His Creation

The personality of the sculptor comes through in the sculpture. Similarly, as Creator, God expresses himself in all he has made, and what he made reveals and declares important things about him. This truth helps us better appreciate why Adam, as representative of humanity, was given the task of naming the animals. The Genesis creation account contains this rather startling passage: "Now the LORD God had formed out of the ground all the wild animals and all the birds in the sky. He brought them to the man to see what he would name them; and whatever the man called each living creature, that was its name" (Gen. 2:19). This passage strikes contemporary readers as somewhat odd, until we understand that for the ancient Hebrews, to "name" something meant much more than it does to modern Americans. It meant to understand it deeply, to know the essence of the thing named. That is why to the Hebrews, and to some cultures today, to name a child is such an important event.

God was bringing his creatures to Adam so that Adam could share in God's knowledge of his creation. Adam was to reflect knowing and understanding the animals the way the Creator knows and understands them. In doing so, he would not only reflect the knowledge and wisdom of his Creator, but he would also know God in a deeper, more profound way. Naming a tiger, for example, would help

Adam understand and appreciate the beauty and power of God's creation. Adam's encounter with an otter, by contrast, would teach him something about the Creator's own playfulness and sense of humor. By extension, then, "naming the animals" is what happens whenever we study God's creation and learn new things about it. It's what botanists do when they discover a new plant species, or what astronomers do when they discover a new galaxy and put a name on it.

Moreover, when we move from Genesis to the New Testament, we learn that creation itself was the work of Jesus Christ. Paul writes in his letter to the Colossians: "For in him all things were created: things in heaven and on earth, visible and invisible, whether thrones or powers or rulers or authorities; all things have been created through him and for him" (Col. 1:16). To study the created world, therefore, is actually to study the works of Christ himself.

Because Christians begin the educational task with the understanding that the entire universe is Christ's creation, learning new subjects is never simply about acquiring more information.

Because Christians begin the educational task with the understanding that the entire universe is Christ's creation, learning new subjects is never simply about acquiring more information. It's a way to know Christ better and more deeply love him. As John Piper notes, "Everything—from the bottom of the oceans to the top of the mountains, from the smallest particle to the biggest star, from the most boring school subject to the most fascinating science, from the ugliest cockroach to the most beautiful human . . . exists to make the greatness of Christ more fully known." A class in cell biology, for instance, isn't just a preparation for the next stage of a premed program; properly understood, it's actually a way to deepen one's relationship with Christ, the creator of cells.

We Are Called to Care for and Develop God's Creation

The creation story tells us that God intended human beings not just to "name" his creation but to cultivate it and develop it. Christians often seem so interested in the serpent and apple episode that they fail to ask an important question of the creation story: What would Adam and Eve have done with their lives if they hadn't sinned and been kicked out of Eden? After all, one suspects that simply eating fruit and naming animals would have grown tedious after a while.

So what was God's original purpose for his image bearers? Genesis 1 and 2 give us a clue: "God blessed them and said to them, 'Be fruitful and increase in number; fill the earth and subdue it. Rule over the fish in the sea and the birds in the sky and over every living creature that moves on the ground'" (Gen. 1:28). And a few verses later: "The LORD God took the man and put him in the Garden of Eden to work it and take care of it" (Gen. 2:15). Many of us have encountered these passages so often that we miss their significance: the God of the universe is actually entrusting his glorious new creation to the care and oversight of frail human beings. It sounds something like a father giving the keys of his new Ferrari convertible to his sixteen-year-old son. Indeed, one of the astounding truths of

Genesis 1 and 2 is that God gives Adam and Eve tremendous responsibilities to rule over and care for his creation.

The notion of human beings as rulers over creation applies to higher education in two important ways. First, a ruler is not a tyrant. The Hebrews clearly distinguished between a conquering tyrant like Nebuchadnezzar and a good monarch such as King David, who ruled for the benefit of his people. As rulers, Christians are called to care for and preserve God's good creation—an important principle in our modern era in which human activity has had such a far-reaching impact on the environment. Because modern society and the environment are complex and intertwined, a Christian college impacts creation care in a variety of ways and disciplines. It may be a biology class seeking to understand the impact of rising temperatures on Amazon biodiversity, or an economics class exploring the impact of family-based agriculture on the environment in rural Africa, or a public policy class seeking the best way to balance resource development and wildlife preservation in the American West. A Christian college education will prepare you to be a better steward of creation, whether that's in your professional career or simply in the shopping choices you make as a consumer.

Second, the good ruler not only cares for the kingdom but actively *develops* it—bringing improvements, solving disputes, and increasing prosperity. And that is the privilege God entrusted to humans. From the initial tending of the Garden in Genesis, humans were expected to bring beneficial changes to creation. Theologians refer to this task as the "cultural mandate"—that God created humans not only to enjoy his creation, but to develop it, even to transform it. Consider the opposite end of the Bible, the book of Revelation. This book tells us that the culmination of God's redemptive work will not be another garden but rather a city—and not an ordinary city, but one with walls decorated with precious jewels, streets of gold, and gardens and vineyards. If Genesis depicts a creation as simple and harmonious as a Bach cello solo, Revelation describes a complex, multilayered creation like a Beethoven symphony.

So how do we get from the Garden to the Heavenly City? By human beings actively and creatively cultivating God's creation. We often associate the word "culture" with particular forms such as art, music, and dance—hence we call a person "cultured" who is knowledgeable about such things. But as Andy Crouch explains in *Culture Making*, culture is simply "what we make of the world." By implication, therefore, everything humans do, from making an omelet to designing a car, is an act of making culture that fulfills God's original good purpose for his creation.

> *Many of your college courses, and particularly your major, will prepare you to assume your God-given role as a fellow cultivator of creation.*

The importance of developing God's creation is reinforced when one moves to the New Testament and the person of Christ—namely, the doctrine of the Incarnation. The fact that Jesus Christ, while fully God, took on actual flesh and blood means that the material stuff of creation is not to be avoided but valued. Christians, of all people, should appreciate the fact that the world Christ chose to inhabit, though fallen, still holds the potential for great beauty and complexity.

One of the purposes of a college education, therefore, is to equip us to engage in and cultivate God's good creation more lovingly and effectively. The study of engineering, for example, helps us to learn how to build bridges that span rivers. Architecture teaches us how to construct more efficient and comfortable buildings. Graphic design teaches us how to create objects that communicate with clarity and aesthetic appeal. Business helps us develop healthy economic relationships that are essential to any complex society. A course in English helps us use language in creative new ways. And the list goes on. Many of your college courses, and particularly your major, will prepare you to assume your God-given role as a fellow cultivator of creation.

The Study of Creation Includes the Insights of Nonbelievers

There is a popular slogan at Christian colleges: "All truth is God's truth, wherever it may be found." Over the next few years, you may grow weary of hearing this remark, but it's true nonetheless. Because God created all that exists and called it good, all aspects of creation are worth studying. Thus, a Christian college does not limit itself to studying only Christian writers and Christian ideas. We study a variety of academic subjects and scholars, even non-Christians— not just to refute their ideas but to learn from them.

How can this be true? One implication of the creation story is the doctrine of "common grace"—that is, that God has liberally sprinkled his grace over all his creation, and the effects of God's grace persist even after the Fall. Even non-Christian scholars can have insights into truths about the universe. The atheistic scientists James Watson and Francis Crick, for example, were the first researchers to discern the structure of DNA. They did so by diligently studying creation, not by reading the Bible. John Calvin likened the non-Christian scholar's situation to that of "a traveler passing through a field at night who in a momentary lightning flash sees far and wide, but the sight vanishes so swiftly that he is plunged again into the darkness of the night before he can take even a step." We may disagree with Calvin over the extent to which the non-Christian is "plunged again into darkness," but his lightning metaphor is helpful nonetheless.

Sigmund Freud, for example, may have been wrong about the general truths of God's personal existence and humanity's divine spark. But his experiments and explorations of the subconscious yield helpful insights into the human psyche for non-Christians and Christians alike. Freud's writings may be potentially threatening to a young Christian raised in a sheltered environment, but they are still worth taking seriously and can teach us valuable truths.

This idea of listening to and learning from those we may disagree with applies not only to thinkers from the past but also to our counterparts in the present. Such a notion is an especially important feature of a Christian college in our politically polarized culture. Examples abound of secular universities clamping down on ideological diversity, either because they deem a dissenting point of view unworthy of consideration, or out of a desire to provide "safe spaces" for students they deem to be emotionally fragile. The Christian college, by contrast, operates from the perspective that all humans are made in God's image. Moreover, the doctrine of common grace says those we disagree with are worth listening to, however misguided we may believe them to be. One Christian university in the Pacific Northwest, for example, intentionally features non-Christian speakers in an annual lecture series in order to provide students with the opportunity to interact with new ideas and expose them to vigorous but civil debate.

Strengthened by the confidence that all truth is God's truth, a Christian college is free to provide students with *emotional* safety but *intellectual* risk. Exposure to new and sometimes uncomfortable ideas is part of what makes a college campus an invigorating place to be.

We Glorify God by Taking Delight in His Creation

Participating in God's creation involves not just the intellect but the emotions. Humans were created to experience the same kind of joy and delight in the creation that the Creator himself experiences. God revels in his creation, enjoys it, and loves it. Genesis 1 informs us repeatedly that God took great delight in his creative activity and called it good. The importance of this truth—God delighting in his creation— is reinforced throughout the Scriptures. In Job 38–41, for example, God tells Job that he plays with large sea creatures; he boasts about the rivers he creates, the storehouses of snow that he keeps, and the understanding he gives to the different creatures.

> *We have been uniquely created to understand, to delight in, and to enjoy the creation the way God does.*

Of all the creatures, Genesis tells us, humans alone were created in God's image. Theologians call this concept the *imago dei*, the image of God. And while theologians continue to debate the full meaning of this expression, they do agree it means we have been uniquely created to understand, to delight in, and to enjoy the creation the way God does.

Here's an analogy: Picture a father painstakingly constructing a swing set for his children. His effort is motivated by the expectation of seeing their joy and hearing their laughter when they jump off the swings and slide down the slide. Their enjoyment of the swing set not only reflects the father's own affinity for play, but it also expresses their gratitude and admiration for his handiwork. Similarly, when we admire the Grand Canyon, kayak a mountain stream, or cook a savory meal, we express the reality of the *imago dei* and bring pleasure to the Creator of these things.

This concept of human beings created to delight in God's creation gives further purpose to a Christian college. That's because the beauty of God's creation is not limited to the natural world; we experience it in human culture as well. Poets, artists, philosophers, and even mathematicians discover and develop parts of creation that delight the imagination and feed the soul. I once saw a documentary about a Princeton mathematician who proved a geometrical concept called Fermat's last theorem. He broke down in tears as he described the moment of discovery and the "indescribable beauty" and simplicity of the proof.

One of the purposes of a Christian college, therefore, is to help us develop the ability not just to understand but to delight in God's physical creation. A child can enjoy Beethoven's Fifth Symphony. But the person who has studied music theory, music history, and the tragic life of Beethoven can appreciate the symphony in a far deeper way. Similarly, the graduate of a course in astronomy can enjoy the beauty of the stars in a deeper way than the person who simply recognizes the Big Dipper in the night sky. Higher education develops our ability to glorify God by enjoying his creation in all of its diversity and depth.

These four insights from the creation story can be summed up in the notion of education as an *intrinsic* good, or good for its own sake. We can think of objects as having either instrumental or intrinsic value. A shovel, for example, is a tool that has instrumental value. We don't mount it on our wall to admire; we use it to dig a hole. The *Mona Lisa*, by contrast, is good for its own sake, not for any use that we would put it to. Similarly, a beautiful sunset is an intrinsic good. We admire it for itself, not for any practical purpose that it could be put to. When it comes to education, society typically views college in instrumental terms: a college education pays off in a more lucrative and satisfying career. Christians, however, begin with the understanding that learning has *intrinsic* value regardless of whatever practical benefits it might produce. God created all things, and he created us in his image to explore and delight in his creation.

It's popular nowadays to turn nouns into verbs. For example, we don't just read a text. Rather, we *text* a colleague on our cell phone, or we *friend* someone on Facebook. In conclusion, it may be helpful to think of *image* as a verb rather than a noun: as Christians, one of our chief callings in life is to "image" God. Clifford Williams, in his book *The Life of the Mind*, coins the term "living largely" to describe our calling as God's image bearers. Too many Christians, he says, live constricted lives. They miss the wideness of experience that comes to those who are open to new possibilities. Living a constricted life is like reading Harlequin romances instead of Toni Morrison or drinking fruit punch rather than French wine. When we live largely, however, we actively look for fresh ways to experience the richness and goodness of God's creation. In other words, we image God better and more deeply as we engage in his creation.

At its most basic level, college prepares you to image God throughout all of life, regardless of the particular major or career you are studying for. God creates; as his image bearer, I subcreate. Studying art and music enables me to be a better creator. Studying history enables me to better understand how humans have cultivated the garden of civilization over time. Every book I read, mathematical equation I wrestle with, or painting I experience expands me and, by extension, my ability to image God. Reading English literature or mastering the cello may not make me love God more, but it gives me *more* to love God *with*.

As we'll see in the next chapter, the world is flawed in some significant ways. But that shouldn't blind us to the goodness that still pervades God's creation and our opportunity as image bearers of God to understand, develop, and delight in that creation. A Christian college education enables us to do that in deeper and richer ways.

A Note on Sources

All Scripture references are from the New International Version. Willimon and Taylor's observation about college students as "money-making machines" is found in *The Abandoned Generation* (Grand Rapids: Eerdmans, 1995), 39. An important analysis of the college student generation is Jean Twenge, *iGen: Why Today's Super-Connected Kids Are Growing Up Less Rebellious, More Tolerant, Less Happy, and Completely Unprepared for Adulthood* (New York: Simon & Schuster, 2017). John Calvin's remark about common grace is found in an article by David Neff, "Why God Enjoys Baseball" (*Christianity Today*, July 8, 2002). Two of the best sources for reading more about the doctrine of creation and education are Andy Crouch, *Culture Making: Recovering Our Creative Calling* (Downers Grove, IL: InterVarsity Press, 2008) and Clifford Williams, *The Life of the Mind* (Ada, MI: Baker Academic, 2002). A more recent book connecting the value of learning to Jesus Christ is Mark Noll, *Jesus Christ and the Life of the Mind* (Grand Rapids: Eerdmans, 2010). John Piper's remark is from Noll, 28.

Among the many helpful recent books on Christian creation care is Steven Bouma-Prediger, *For the Beauty of the Earth: A Christian Vision for Creation Care* (Ada, MI: Baker Academic, 2010). A helpful treatment of intellectual culture in the modern university is Greg Lukianoff and Jonathan Haidt, *The Coddling of the American Mind: How Good Intentions and Bad Ideas Are Setting Up a Generation for Failure* (New York: Penguin, 2018).

The discussion of learning as an intrinsic good comes largely from Williams, *Life of the Mind*, chapter two. Also, I am indebted to David Brisben, former chair of the biblical studies department at John Brown University, for many of the formative ideas in this chapter.

Questions for Reflection and Discussion

1. If every college course is an opportunity to know God better, why is it often difficult to be motivated to learn and study?

2. What is a particular way that the "cultural mandate" would apply to your major?

3. Is it possible for Christian colleges to both equip students to "delight in God's creation" and to prepare them for a career? Why or not?

4. What is one course you are taking this semester that will enable you to "live largely"? How, specifically, will it do so?

5. Could a non-Christian pursue education for its intrinsic value? Why or why not?

4 NOT THE WAY IT'S SUPPOSED TO BE

The Doctrine of the Fall

THE previous chapter explained the purpose of a Christian college in helping us understand, develop, and delight in God's good creation. Unfortunately, events around us often have provided more vivid reminders of ways the world does not represent God's benevolent purposes. There was the onset of the COVID-19 pandemic, which wreaked havoc on everything from the global economy to weddings and graduation ceremonies. Then in spring 2020, there was the horrific video footage of a black man in Minneapolis being killed by a white police officer—a vivid demonstration of the racism, injustice, and division that continue to pervade modern society.

George Floyd's brutal murder and the ensuing protests brought to mind an insightful and still relevant movie from a generation ago called *Grand Canyon*. It used the physical feature of the Grand Canyon as a metaphor for the racial and social divisions in America, and it depicted two Los Angeles families as they sought to bridge the divide. In the opening scene a wealthy, white Los Angeles businessman, played by Kevin Kline, attempts to take a shortcut home from a Lakers game late at night, only to have his BMW break down in a run-down neighborhood. He calls for a tow truck, but before it arrives, Kline is surrounded by a group of black teenagers who plan to steal his car. The tow truck driver, an older black man played by Danny Glover, arrives during a tense standoff between Kevin Kline and the youths. Glover talks with the head of the gang, asking that he be permitted to tow the car—and Kevin Kline—to safety.

At the end of their conversation, Glover exclaims to the youth, "Man, the world ain't supposed to work like this. Maybe you don't know that, but this ain't the way it's supposed to be. I'm supposed to be able to do my job without asking you if I can. That dude's supposed to be able to wait with his car without you ripping him off." He concludes with the memorable line, "Everything's supposed to be different than what it is."

Glover is referring to several examples from the film's opening scene: in a world "the way it's supposed to be," cities aren't divided between white and black neighborhoods. Wealth isn't divided between a few haves and a host of have-nots. Urban youths don't form gangs and resort to crime and violence as their only way to escape poverty. Cars don't break down at inopportune times. In fact, Glover's soliloquy aptly sums up the biblical doctrine of the Fall: sin entered the world through Adam and Eve, and its effects spread throughout all God's creation. What we see around us today is a distorted version of the beautiful, harmonious world God created. In this chapter, we'll return to the biblical story of the Fall, then explore its implications for education.

Genesis 3 tells a story that is familiar to most of us in Western culture. God places Adam and Eve in the Garden of Eden and commands them not to eat from the "tree of the knowledge of good and evil." Which, of course, is exactly what they do.

> When the woman saw that the fruit of the tree was good for food and pleasing to the eye, and also desirable for gaining wisdom, she took some and ate it. She also gave some to her husband, who was with her, and he ate it. Then the eyes of both of them were opened, and they realized they were naked; so they sewed fig leaves together and made coverings for themselves. (Gen. 3:6–7)

I recall encountering this story in Sunday school when I was growing up. The basic lesson was that sin created a gulf between humanity and God and made it necessary for Jesus Christ to die for our sins to restore that relationship. What I didn't understand at the time was that the Fall, as theologians call it, disrupted not only human beings' relationship with God but in some mysterious way impacted all of God's creation—all the way to viruses that mutate and destroy hundreds of thousands of people. As Michael Wittmer observes in his book *Heaven Is a Place on Earth*, "Adam's sin did not just affect

Sin entered the world through Adam and Eve, and its effects spread throughout all God's creation. What we see around us today is a distorted version of the beautiful, harmonious world God created.

him but, like a stone tossed into a pond, rippled out until it had destroyed the entire world."

First and most obviously, Adam and Eve's disobedience corrupted human relationships. Suddenly they realized they were naked and sought to cover themselves with fig leaves. Soon the finger-pointing began. When God asked Adam if he ate from the tree, Adam replied, "The woman you put here with me—she gave me some fruit from the tree, and I ate it" (3:12). Things soon grew worse. Their son Cain, jealous over the favor that God showed to his brother Abel, killed Abel and was forced to flee for his life. In fact, the next few chapters depict the ripple effects of the Fall throughout human society, until the writer of Genesis states in chapter six: "The LORD saw how great the wickedness of the human race had become on the earth, and that every inclination of the thoughts of the human heart was only evil all the time. The LORD regretted that he had made human beings on the earth, and his heart was deeply troubled" (6:5–6). Quite the contrast from the Creator who delighted in the goodness of his creation.

Adam and Eve's disobedience altered not only human society but the natural world as well. After Adam ate the forbidden fruit, God said to him, "Cursed is the ground because of you; through painful toil you will eat food from it all the days of your life. It will produce thorns and thistles for you" (3:17–18). The pleasurable cultivation of the Garden that was Adam's original task was now reduced to the drudgery of hacking at hard soil to extract some edible crops. Even the animal world became implicated in the mess. In Genesis 6, God sent the flood not just to do away with humans but also with the rest of creation: "So the LORD said, 'I will wipe from the face of the earth the human race I have created—and with them the animals, the birds and the creatures that move along the ground—for I regret that I have made them'" (6:7).

In the New Testament, the apostle Paul aptly describes the cosmic nature of the Fall when he writes, "[T]he whole creation has been groaning as in the pains of childbirth right up to the present time" (Rom. 8:22). In some mysterious way, all of creation has become disfigured by the effects of the Fall, so what we see around us today is, as Danny Glover remarked, "not the way it's supposed to be."

Much more can be said about the Christian doctrine of the Fall. Indeed, volumes have been written over the centuries exploring how evil relates to divine sovereignty and human free will, how "original sin" spread, whether death in the natural world is a result of the Fall, and a host of other related issues. You will probably navigate these turbulent waters at some point in your college career. Our purpose, however, is not to discuss the Fall in exhaustive detail but to look at Christian education through the lens of this foundational belief. So what does the Fall have to do with college? Here are some implications.

The Fall and the Goodness of Creation

First, it's important to consider what the Fall does *not* mean: the evil that we see in the world is *not* consonant with the creation itself. The goodness of God's creation persists despite its disfigurement by sin. One author has likened evil to a parasite on creation. That's a good analogy, since, like a tapeworm in a dog's intestine, evil depends on a preexisting good for its very existence. Moreover, as C. S. Lewis noted in *Mere Christianity*, it is the highest parts of creation that have the potential for the greatest evil: "The better stuff a creature is made of—the cleverer and stronger and freer it is—then the better it will be if it goes right, but also the worse it will be if it goes wrong."

> "The better stuff a creature is made of—the cleverer and stronger and freer it is—then the better it will be if it goes right, but also the worse it will be if it goes wrong."

This is important to keep in mind because sometimes Christians seem to identify evil with certain parts of creation itself, rather than as a corruption of creation, and then they avoid those aspects of creation altogether. For some, it is sex, or certain foods and drinks, or "worldly amusements" such as movies and cards, or politics. Yet many of the evils that Christians perceive in the world are actually distortions of some of creation's basic goods. God's good gift of sex becomes twisted into adultery or prostitution. Wine is distorted into drunkenness. Even the existence of a corrupt dictatorship depends on the prior good of political institutions that God established.

As noted in the previous chapter, one of the basic doctrines of Christianity is the Incarnation—that in the person of Jesus Christ, God took on human flesh and lived an earthly existence. As Christians through the centuries have pointed out, the Incarnation implies that the basic stuff of creation is good, and even though it is corrupted, it is still redeemable. Furthermore, God's common grace continues to sustain his creation, and Scripture tells us that the Holy

Spirit actively restrains evil in the world. Thus, some significant vestiges of creation's goodness still persist. All parts of creation, from art to science to law to politics, merit our attention and our engagement. Nothing is irredeemably corrupt. Political science, for example, enables Christians to study politics as the proper and effective use of power—as part of God's gifting of his creation, despite the distorted ends that humans have often used it for. As Christians, our task is not to avoid certain subjects for fear of contamination, but to engage them as part of God's blessings on his creation.

The "Hermeneutics of Suspicion"

Because of the Fall, however, Christians must approach academic life with a healthy dose of skepticism. If the doctrine of the Fall teaches us anything, it's that human beings can be selfish, corrupt, mistaken, and self-deluded—even when they are trying to do good. Christians call this notion human depravity, and it affects scholarship in two important ways. First, because of our understanding of human nature, we would do well to apply what one scholar called a "hermeneutics of suspicion" to our studies. This rather ominous phrase simply means that we recognize all humans have biases. Thus, intentionally or not, their interpretation of the evidence can be distorted by their

> *As Christians, we should approach any truth claim with both generosity and suspicion— whether that truth claim comes from Sigmund Freud or your local pastor.*

desires. So as Christians, we should approach any truth claim with both generosity *and* suspicion—whether that truth claim comes from Sigmund Freud or your local pastor.

When I was growing up, for example, I learned from Christian historians that America was founded as a Christian nation. Later I read the primary documents for myself and discovered that a variety of secular and Christian influences contributed to the founding of America. The Christians who advocated the notion of America's Christian origins were not bad people; they simply allowed their good intentions to color their approach to history. The same dynamic occurs, to a greater or lesser extent, in all disciplines. Like speculators who rush in to buy Florida real estate, convinced that the boom market will never end, scholars throughout history have made breathless assertions about the "indisputable truth" of their findings, only to be proven wrong later. We need to approach any subject, therefore, with a healthy sense of skepticism.

Second, as fallen humans, we need to apply that same suspicion not only to new ideas we encounter but to those we consider to be on "our side," culturally and politically. Today's polarized political culture, combined with the fragmentation of the mainstream media, has produced a phenomenon known as the

> *One of the most valuable qualities that Christian education can instill, therefore, is a sense of intellectual humility—the ability to acknowledge, "I might be wrong about this."*

echo chamber: Americans increasingly associate—both physically and in social media—with others who are like them, and they gravitate toward news sources that reinforce their own points of view. The result is that proponents on both sides of issues can grow deaf to—or simply unaware of—any reasonable perspectives from those on the other side of religious, political, or social issues. Perhaps you have encountered this phenomenon when you have visited extended family for Thanksgiving dinner.

One of the most valuable qualities that Christian education can instill, therefore, is a sense of intellectual humility—the ability to acknowledge, "I might be wrong about this." An awareness of our own fallenness and capacity for self-delusion enables us to listen to others and function as teachable members of a college community. The Fall teaches us to be wary of others' truth claims, but it also reminds us to be modest in our own assertions and open to learning from others. A Bible professor may not be infallible, but her years of study of ancient culture and languages mean that her insights are worth considering when she challenges my assumptions about Genesis. A sociology professor who talks about structural racism should prompt not defensiveness but curiosity and an openness to new perspectives.

The Complexity of Evil

For the Christian, one of the purposes of education is to help us understand the subtle, complex, and at times *systemic* effects of the Fall not just on individuals but on our world. Sin has a way of working its way into the very systems and structures of our lives and, indeed, entire societies. It has a pernicious tendency to make the abnormal and the monstrous seem normal, and that can make understanding the world a complicated task requiring careful study. Consider, for example, the following letter sent by a businessman to his boss concerning a shortage of muffles and ovens:

> At this time three double-muffle ovens are in operation, with a capacity of 250 per day. Furthermore, currently under construction are five triple-muffle ovens with a daily capacity of 800. Today and in the next few days, two eight-muffle ovens, each with a daily capacity of 800, will come on consignment, redirected from Mogilew. Mr. K said that this number of muffles is not yet sufficient; we should deliver more ovens as quickly as possible.

This letter seems to describe the ordinary stuff of business—buying and selling products, keeping up with demand, and so on. Except that in this particular example, the businessman is an employee of the German industrial firm *Topf und Sohne*, and the "products" are crematory ovens for Auschwitz death camp. The "capacity" refers to the number of human beings that can be cremated per day. This normalizing of evil seems rather monstrous to us today, but if you had been a German worker in the 1940s and had grown up in a society steeped in German racial doctrines and the importance of obeying authority, would you have recognized it as such? Many German Christians did not.

What enables us to recognize the situation just described as evil is not just a Christian belief in the value of all human beings but also the benefit of historical perspective and hindsight. We do not, however, have historical perspective on our own society, nor enough social distance to recognize the subtle ways the Fall infiltrates our own system of life. For example, as Christians who believe that all people are made in God's image, we believe all human beings should have an equal opportunity for success in life. But we live in a society in which the playing field is often severely slanted. My children grew up in East Grand Rapids, Michigan, where 95 percent of the kids graduate from the local high school and 86 percent go on to college. At a school district just two miles away, 70 percent of the kids graduate from high school and only 33 percent go on to college. There are many complicated reasons for such disparities, but they reflect at least in part an American educational system in which the benefits and services flow toward those communities with greater economic resources and in which the systemic effects of racism still persist.

Or consider the global economic structures that shape our lives. In the 1800s, northern Christians in the United States condemned slavery in the South. But they also purchased cotton products that made slave labor in the South such a profitable enterprise. Once again, with the advantage of history, we can recognize the northerners' culpability in the institution of slavery. But without a careful study of economics and sociology in modern society, we may fail to notice economic systems today that encourage injustice in other parts of the world. Does my purchase of Nike running shoes, for example, contribute to the exploitation of a worker in a sweatshop in Malaysia? Do my consumer choices contribute indirectly to the degradation of the environment? Those actions would hardly rank up there with producing ovens for Auschwitz, but they're participation in a flawed system nonetheless—and they're often difficult to discern.

One of the key questions that a student at a Christian college must ask is, "How is the cultural arena that my major is preparing me for *not* the way it's supposed to be?" Answering that question, however, can be difficult when we swim in the same cultural waters we are attempting to study. One purpose of Christian education, therefore, is to develop the ability to recognize the complex effects of the Fall on creation. Condemning genocide is relatively easy; understanding subtle and complex systemic evils is not. Doing so requires an understanding of history, theology, social sciences, and other subjects. And it requires a thorough knowledge of your own major in light of a Christian worldview.

One Size Doesn't Fit All

As with human society in general, college life demonstrates an inter-mingling of the good of creation with the corruption of the Fall. Take a typical college soccer game, for example. As we have seen, play is rooted in the doctrine of creation. A soccer game allows human beings to image God by delighting in creation, and it applies the cultural mandate by developing the human impulse to play into a particular structure where athletic creativity and coopera-tion can thrive. Moreover, friendly athletic competition can con-tribute to human community. Yet the athletic beauty of a soccer game this side of heaven comes accompanied by the baggage of the Fall. Dazzling saves are matched by slide tackles from behind and taunting of opponents. Spectators cheer their team—until the first questionable call, after which the cheers turn into angry berating of the referees.

Other aspects of college life demonstrate the same mixture of goodness and fallenness. Facebook was actually created on a college campus (Harvard), and Instagram enables college students to widen their social circles to span the globe. But scholars have also documented the rise in depression, loneliness, and suicide rates that has coincided with the growth of social media. And, of course, a significant number of college students, on both secular and Christian campuses, corrupt the intrinsic good of academic learning by plagiarizing papers from the Internet or cheating on exams. Once again, the evil—cheating—attaches itself like a parasite to the prior good of Christian learning. All these areas, however, are peripheral to the main focus of this book—the college classroom. So how does the Fall affect academic life in particular? Actually, the answer to that question is fairly complicated.

> *One purpose of Christian education . . . is to develop the ability to recognize the complex effects of the Fall on creation. Condemning genocide is relatively easy; understanding subtle and complex systemic evils is not.*

Christians generally agree that sin corrupts not just the human will and emotions but also the mind. The question is to what extent. In other words, how does the Fall affect the average person's ability to think and to understand the world correctly? Or to put it more bluntly, does your chemistry textbook bear the marks of the Fall?

It's a question that Christian theologians have debated for centuries, and it's one that bears directly on our lives at a Christian college.

Some have believed that non-Christian thinkers are so darkened in their understanding that they cannot think or write (or paint or compose) correctly. Academic disciplines depend on prior assumptions, and in some disciplines those assumptions are biased against religious belief. For example, Richard Lewontin, a Harvard biologist, once confessed his guiding faith commitment in scientific materialism.

> We have a prior commitment . . . to materialism. It is not that the methods and institutions of science somehow compel us to accept a material explanation of the phenomenal world, but on the contrary, that we are forced by our a priori adherence to material causes to create an apparatus of investigation and a set of concepts that produce material explanations, no matter how counterintuitive, no matter how mystifying to the uninitiated. Moreover, that materialism is absolute, for we cannot allow a Divine Foot in the door.

Lewontin's materialistic stance is one that many modern scientists share, though rarely do they acknowledge their assumptions as honestly as he does.

Even the arts bear the heavy imprint of the Fall. A decade ago, Aliza Shvarts, an art student at Yale University, presented a rather unusual senior project: she claimed to have artificially inseminated herself with sperm, then "performed" what she called "repeated self-induced miscarriages." Her purpose, she said, was to raise questions about society and the body, namely the stigma that

society attaches to the term "miscarriage." One Ivy League professor described Shvarts as "an imaginative and worthy heir" to Manet.
To many, however, especially those in the Christian community, her
exhibit was simply evidence of the misguided nature of modern art.

Faced with countless examples of the Fall's effects on culture,
Christians often take an oppositional stance toward science and
art. But our task is more complicated than that, since as we have
seen, often unbelievers have insights from which we need to learn. It
would be easy simply to dismiss Charles Darwin or Sigmund Freud
as unredeemable opponents of Christianity, or to use Ms. Shvart's
aborted babies as an excuse to condemn modern art altogether. But
doing so would be to shirk our duty to understand all of God's creation and deprive ourselves of possible new insights. Rather, in any
academic discipline, we must ask questions such as these: To what
extent does this subject rely on unspoken assumptions? Which of
those assumptions overlap with a Christian worldview? How does
common grace affect this subject? The writer of the chemistry textbook, after all, may believe that all of life can be reduced to mere
chemical processes. But that does not prevent the Christian from
learning about ionic and covalent bonds from the book.

Simply put, the Fall affects the various subjects that we study in
different ways. What the Christian student needs above all, therefore, is *flexibility* in approaching human thought and culture. Let
me explain. Andy Crouch's book *Culture Making: Recovering Our
Creative Calling* contains an insightful chapter entitled "Gestures
and Postures." Human beings make a variety of bodily gestures in
the course of a day, and over time gestures that are repeated develop
postures. A posture is the body's default position, the one that we

take when we aren't paying attention to it. My daughter, for example, is a ballet dancer, and her countless hours in the studio have resulted in a light, graceful walking gait. My wife's grandfather, a farmer, spent so many years picking vegetables that when I met him as an old man, his back was permanently inclined at an angle.

Crouch observes that in the cultural realm, too, gestures can become postures—a phenomenon demonstrated in history by American Christians. A century ago, conservative Christians so frequently condemned worldly ideas and behaviors that their gesture became an instinctive posture of *condemnation* toward secular culture and ideas. These conservatives were followed by a generation of Christians in the mid-twentieth century who rejected the separatism of their parents. They sought instead to *critique* culture by analyzing cultural products from a Christian worldview perspective.

In the 1960s and 1970s, evangelicals launched the Christian youth culture and CCM, or contemporary Christian music. They sought to *copy* culture by importing the forms of rock music and pop culture into the safe bubble of the Christian subculture. For many of us today, the self-consciously Christian and derivative nature of CCM bands, with their T-shirts and Christian Woodstocks, may seem a bit cheesy. A common posture for Christians today, Crouch observes, is cultural *consumption* when it comes to music, books, films, or technology. That is, they uncritically watch films, surf the web, or maintain their Facebook site with little attention to how such behaviors may be subtly affecting them or their communities.

Crouch's insights apply to academic life as well. All the postures Crouch describes are potentially appropriate; it just depends on the subject. Take the study of film, for example. One of the primary goals of Christian education is to produce mature, *thinking* students who can evaluate the world around them from a Christian perspective. And that applies to the films we watch. But only when doing so is appropriate. You could, of course, apply *critique* to the classic *Shrek* films by analyzing them as a commentary on the "princess" motif in Western literature and as a parody of modern culture's preoccupation with external physical appearance. But if you do, you'll probably just annoy those around you who are busy laughing at the earthy jokes and witty dialogue. It's probably best just to sit back and enjoy—or *consume—Shrek* as a funny film.

Other films, such as *The Social Network*, may require a combination of both consumption and critique. Its scenes depicting Harvard student life and sharp dialogues are very entertaining, but the film also raises deep questions about technology and human community that merit critique and analysis from a Christian perspective. Still others, such as *Twelve Years a Slave*, may be painful to watch, but they merit our attention because of the disturbing subjects for moral reflection that they raise. And finally, there are plenty of films that simply deserve *condemnation* as worthy of neither entertainment nor reflection.

The same variability of approaches applies to other academic subjects as well. The college classroom is most often associated with *critique*—understood not simply as criticism but rather as the attempt to understand and analyze a subject in its proper context. But many intellectual and cultural products also are meant to be consumed, not just analyzed. We can take critique too far if we miss the enjoyment of an eloquent poem, a beautiful painting, or even an elegant scientific theory. Shakespeare's plays merit critique and analysis, but we would also do well to *copy* them—that is, to have Shakespeare's marvelous feel for words and the rhythm of language leaven our own writing. Physics students should seek to understand and analyze Einstein's theories, but they should also emulate Einstein's ability to grasp the simple concept amid the complexities.

Finally, in a world darkened by the Fall, Christians must retain *condemnation* as an option. For example, Hitler's *Mein Kampf* can be studied as a window into the culture of early-twentieth-century Germany, but ultimately its pernicious racial doctrines deserve our condemnation. In other words, it's often helpful to frame one's study of a subject around this guiding question: What is the most appropriate posture, or combination of postures, to assume in relation to this particular subject or artifact?

As Christian scholars, our approach to a subject will vary depending on the nature of that subject and its connection to the Fall. It comes down to knowing when to condemn, when to copy, when to critique, and when to consume; and the answers are rarely straightforward. Ultimately, Christian education depends on wisdom rather than on a prescribed formula. It would be easier, of course, to adopt a single posture to govern our approach to academics. But that would also be shallower and much less interesting. God calls us to study his world in all of its beauty and its fallenness. Doing so requires a robust approach to education and a nimbleness of mind to adopt different stances in different situations.

> *Ultimately, Christian education depends on wisdom rather than on a prescribed formula.*

A Note on Sources

The most thorough recent treatment of the doctrine of the Fall is Cornelius Plantinga, *Not the Way It's Supposed to Be: A Breviary of Sin* (Grand Rapids: Eerdmans, 1995). Wittmer's quote on the extensive effects of Adam's sin is found in Michael Wittmer, *Heaven Is a Place on Earth: Why Everything You Do Matters to God* (Grand Rapids: Zondervan, 2004), 173. C. S. Lewis is quoted in Cornelius Plantinga, *Engaging God's World* (Grand Rapids: Eerdmans, 2002), 53. The *Topf und Sohne* letter can be found online at the Holocaust History Project, https://phdn.org/archives/holocaust -history.org/. Richard Lewontin is quoted in Plantinga, *Engaging God's World*, 68. The description of Aliza Shvartz is in Jacob Appel, "The Value of Controversial Art," *Washington Post* (May 8, 2008. Crouch's discussion of gestures and postures is found in Andy Crouch, *Culture Making* (Downers Grove, IL: InterVarsity Press, 2008), chap. 5. All Scripture citations are from the New International Version.

Questions for Reflection and Discussion

1. Why are "systemic" evils often so difficult to detect and to combat?

2. What practices of modern Christians do you think Christians a century from now will criticize?

3. What would be a specific example of how your own major is impacted by the Fall?

4. Which posture toward culture has been the most common in your own background?

5. How does one determine which posture to adopt in a particular academic or cultural setting?

5   BROADCASTING MOZART

The Doctrine of Redemption

So far we have explored two main acts of the Christian story and their implications for college: all things were created good by God, and all things have been marred by the Fall. Here's part three of the story: God in Christ is working to redeem all of his creation and restore it to the way it was supposed to be. That doesn't necessarily mean all people will be redeemed. Humans have free will, and therefore they have the ability to reject God. But the rest of creation doesn't have a choice in the matter. According to the Bible, it will be restored to its original goodness, and God's people will play an important role in that restoration.

As with the doctrine of the Fall, many of us grow up hearing so much about the notion of redemption that it becomes commonplace to us. Redemption, I learned when I was younger, basically meant "accepting Jesus into your heart so you can go to heaven." While personal salvation is an important part of the story, there's much more to it. The doctrine of redemption is marvelous in its complexity and its implications for all of creation—and ultimately for our understanding of a college education. Indeed, one could argue that our notion of a college education will be as large or as small as our understanding of redemption. A weak notion of redemption has sometimes led Christians to treat college as simply a training session for evangelism or missions. It has also been understood as training for a "secular" career to pay the bills for those Christians who are involved in "real" ministry. But if we have a broader understanding of redemption, college becomes rich with virtually endless possibilities. This chapter will briefly sketch a robust biblical doctrine of redemption, then explore its implications for Christian education.

We'll begin by returning to the story of the Fall in Genesis 3. Immediately after Adam and Eve received the penalty for their disobedience (and creation in general is cursed), God set out fixing things by making "garments of skin" to clothe their nakedness. By Genesis 12, God had selected one person in particular, Abraham, to establish a beachhead of redemption for the human race. God told Abraham, "All peoples on earth will be blessed through you" (12:3). In other words, Abraham's descendants, the nation of Israel, were to be a model of a human society that functions the way things are supposed to be. The Israelites had a term for this—*shalom*—which we often translate as "peace." However, as Cornelius Plantinga explains, *shalom* meant a lot more to the Israelites than just an absence of conflict: "In the Bible, shalom means universal flourishing, wholeness, and delight—a rich state of affairs in which natural needs are satisfied and natural gifts fruitfully employed, all under the arch of God's love."

The Old Testament prophets hinted at this state of shalom that would encompass both the human and natural worlds. Isaiah exclaimed, "The desert and the parched land will be glad; the wilderness will rejoice and blossom" (35:1). Later, the text states, "They will build houses and dwell in them; they will plant vineyards and eat their fruit. . . . The wolf and the lamb will feed together, and the lion will eat straw like the ox" (65:21, 25). Someday, the prophets proclaimed, all creation will be made right and things will once again be the way God created them to be.

The incarnation of Jesus Christ, of course, is the key act in the biblical drama of redemption. In the person of Jesus, God takes on human form, accepts the penalty for sin on the cross, and conquers Satan and death through the resurrection. Christ establishes his church, a people who will be the key agents in extending Christ's victory over sin to the entire creation. Paul sums up the cosmic significance of Christ's work in his letter to the Colossians: "God was pleased to have all his fullness dwell in him, and through him to reconcile to himself all things, whether things on earth or things in heaven, by making peace through his blood, shed on the cross" (1:19–20).

The redemption story doesn't end with the establishment of the church; rather, it culminates in John's vision of a new heaven and a new earth in the book of Revelation. He writes,

> I saw the Holy City, the new Jerusalem, coming down out of heaven from God, prepared as a bride beautifully dressed for her husband. And I heard a loud voice from the throne saying, "Look! God's dwelling place is now among the people, and he will dwell with them. . . . There will be no more death or mourning or crying or pain, for the old order of things has passed away." (21:2–4)

Between Christ's victory over death on the cross and this consummation foretold by John, we as Christians live "between the times," extending the effects of redemption and nudging creation closer to its consummation in Christ.

So what does all this mean for our daily lives here on earth? To understand that, it can be helpful to consider what Jesus meant when he talked about the kingdom of God. American Christians often have misinterpreted this phrase in one of two ways. First, they take Jesus's remark that "the kingdom of God is within you" to mean that the kingdom of God is primarily a matter of having one's inward state redeemed and focused on God. Second, Christians sometimes equate the kingdom of God solely with the future state of heaven, and thus they look at the present life as just some sort of waiting stage before real life begins. As the old gospel hymn puts it: "This world is not my home, I'm just a passin' through." A more biblical way of thinking about the kingdom of God, however, is as a *condition* rather than a location. That is, when Jesus talks about the kingdom of God, he is referring to the active exercise of God's kingly office, which is partially in place in creation now but which will ultimately extend to all of creation, just as it did at the beginning of time.

Albert Wolters employs a helpful analogy to communicate this point: On June 6, 1944, in an event known as D-Day, the armies of the United States and Great Britain established a beachhead in Nazi-occupied northern France. This crucial victory paved the way for the eventual liberation of all Western Europe from the control of Germany. But the final victory did not come until the fall of Berlin on May 8, 1945. As Christians, we can think of Christ's death and resurrection as our D-Day, providing the key turning point in the war against Satan and evil. But the ultimate victory will not come until Christ's second coming. In the meantime, we are engaged in multiple ways in extending the restoration of Christ's rule throughout creation.

Here's a way to visualize the concept. As Christians, we sometimes envision our lives as divided into "sacred" and "secular" compartments, like this:

church family personal life	**the "sacred," Kingdom of God**
politics business art school sports entertainment	**the "secular," Kingdom of the World**

Thus, when we go to church, read the Bible, or relate to others, we are engaging in "Christian" life, but when we watch a film or go to work, we are just engaging in "normal" life.

In a proper understanding of the world and God's intention for it, however, there is no such thing as just normal life. Every part of creation is involved in this endeavor to extend Christ's reign over all his creation. Thus, we can visualize this scenario a better way:

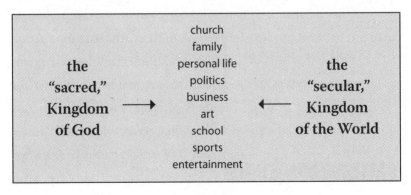

When we apply our calling as Christians to our careers in business, or to the political process, God's reign is extended more completely over creation.

Obviously, the implications of this view of redemption for college are vast. In fact, most Christian colleges would describe their main purpose as preparing students to function as effective agents of redemption throughout all creation. Here are three particular ways redemption relates to education.

Redeeming Your Academic Discipline

Most specifically, we can look at our academic subjects themselves as objects of redemption.

Christians sometimes remark that "only people are eternal." But that's not necessarily the case. In *Culture Making*, Andy Crouch points out the theological implications of John's vision of the Heavenly City in Revelation, which we discussed in Chapter Three. The city, as described by John, is full of cultural artifacts that have been refined and perfected. The city walls consist of jewels—natural artifacts that have been refined by human culture. The city itself, the prophet Isaiah foretells in chapter 60, will be filled with "the glory of the nations." In Isaiah's prophetic vision, not just "Christian" stuff but the best products of human culture—the camels of desert tribes, the swift ships of Tarshish, the beautifully hewn timbers of Lebanon—make a grand processional to the heavenly city. The reader can almost picture a Disney World ride in which every nation displays an idealized form of its most characteristic product, except that in this case the products are real, not plastic or paper-mache.

In a certain sense, then, not just people but *things* have eternal value. Theologian Richard Mouw says, "The final vision of the city is one filled . . . not just with redeemed persons from every cultural background, but with redeemed human culture too." But the key word there is *redeemed*. Human culture must be redeemed and refined before it is suitable for eternity. Such an understanding can revolutionize our approach to college, since much of college life consists of studying and producing cultural goods. A good question to ask ourselves, therefore, when dealing with any cultural prod-

> *Most Christian colleges would describe their main purpose as preparing students to function as effective agents of redemption throughout all creation.*

uct in college is, What would it take for this object, or subject of study, to make it into the heavenly city?

What would it mean to "redeem" your subject of study in college? How about as an art major? Rather than just condemning modern art as corrupt, the Christian artist seeks to "redeem" the medium of art itself, to make it the way it was supposed to be and suitable for the heavenly city. We do so by creating artwork that expresses the human condition in all its beauty, complexity, and at times perhaps even its ugliness. That doesn't mean that redeemed art should depict Mary and the baby Jesus, or cozy cottages nestled beside babbling brooks. It may not convey a clear subject at all. Makoto Fujimura, a

Christian artist in New York City, creates visually stunning abstract art using minerals he pulverizes into various pigments. One of his purposes is to "redeem" the medium of abstract art.

Redemption of this sort is more easily visualized in a hands-on major such as studio art. But what about a more abstract area of study such as history? At some point in your academic career, you will not only learn about history but also *do* history yourself. And when you do, it will be helpful to ask questions such as: In what ways does the discipline of history bear the marks of the Fall? Have historians at times distorted their accounts or failed to tell the whole story? Have they even falsified their evidence, or stolen material from other scholars? How can Christians "redeem" the study of history? That is, how can we produce historical scholarship that is rich, profound, accurate, and engaging? If we assume that real events will occur in the heavenly city, then it's likely that there will be historians there to record and interpret those events. How are you as a student preparing yourself to write the kind of history—or compose poetry, or conduct scientific experiments—that will make it into eternity? Part of our task as cultural beings is to redeem the cultural products that have been corrupted by the Fall, and college is a great place to begin doing that.

> *Part of our task as cultural beings is to redeem the cultural products that have been corrupted by the Fall, and college is a great place to begin doing that.*

Redeeming the World through Your Discipline

For most students, the purpose of college is not necessarily to "redeem" their major but to have that major prepare them to live effectively in the world. This is the most obvious way that redemption applies to higher education. As Christians, we can and should study our disciplines from a Christian perspective, and some students will be called to devote their lives to that task. But most students will be called to use their future profession to make a difference in the world. The English major will use her education to open the eyes of a sixth-grader to the power of written prose. The nursing major will learn to relieve physical suffering, while the art student will use his sculptures to bring beauty to corners of creation where it did not exist before.

So how exactly do we go about changing the world? Actually, the notion of redeeming culture has been the subject of a good deal of discussion and disagreement among Christians. One approach, championed in the late twentieth century by Charles Colson, begins with the assumption that cultures are shaped primarily by *ideas*—in the case of modern culture, ideas such as materialism, moral relativism, and postmodernism. Our job as Christians, therefore, is to be active in the public square in championing a Christian worldview and working to change the dominant ideas and institutions of society.

Other Christians, such as Shane Claiborne or Bryan Stevenson, focus instead on obeying Christ's teachings to minister to the poor and oppressed in society and working to establish racial justice in the United States and abroad. Jesus was not a "cultural warrior," they argue, but he devoted his life to ministering to the outcasts of society. His followers are called to do the same. Others, like Andy Crouch, encourage Christians to engage in "culture making," arguing that the best way to change culture is not by combating it but by making new and better cultural goods. The iPhone, after all, did not have to search and destroy those old flip phones; it was simply a better product.

Finally, Christian sociologist James Davison Hunter has criticized such attempts to change culture as naïve and misguided. Cultures, Hunter argues, change slowly and imperceptibly over centuries, and they do so through the influence of cultural elites and institutions—not through the work of ordinary people arguing their ideas, helping the poor, or making culture. The best that Christians can hope for, according to Hunter, is to exercise a "faithful presence" in society, as the Israelites did as exiles in Babylon, and not worry about trying to change the culture.

Obviously, this debate is more complex than I am describing here, and advocates on all sides have some basis in Scripture. Perhaps a helpful way to envision our cultural task is to consider the example of Jesus. When we look at how Christ interacted with the world in his day, several cultural approaches emerge.

- **Proclamation:** Sometimes Jesus publicly proclaimed the good news of the kingdom and his role in it. As he announced in the synagogue in Nazareth, "The Spirit of the Lord is on me, because he has anointed me to proclaim good news to the poor" (Luke 4:18).

- **Ministry to the poor:** Jesus spent much of his time meeting the physical needs of "the least of these" in society through healing the sick, feeding the hungry, and other acts of compassion.
- **Crossing cultural and ethnic barriers:** In his conversation with the Samaritan woman at the well and at his dinner at the home of the tax collector, Jesus crossed the barriers of Jewish society by associating with people considered "unacceptable" by the religious leaders of his day.
- **Withdrawal:** At times, Jesus withdrew from the crowds to focus on his own relationship with God or to mentor his inner circle of disciples.
- **Active resistance:** At times, Jesus intentionally and aggressively opposed the cultural system of his day, such as when he healed people on the Sabbath and drove the money changers out of the temple.
- **Passive nonresistance:** In contrast to his aggressive resistance, Jesus could be surprisingly passive in his response to culture—most notably during his trial and crucifixion in which he offered no reply or resistance to his accusers.

What is clear from the example of Jesus, therefore, is that no single approach to interacting with culture is sufficient. As we noted in relation to the Fall, Christians should be adept at a variety of ways of acting for good in the world, and they should know when each approach is appropriate. That is why, ultimately, Christian colleges equip students not just with knowledge or skills but with *wisdom*.

Christians must excel in a wide variety of areas and have a depth of insight about their world to understand what stance is most appropriate at a given time.

In sum, Christians are called to be active in culture in a variety of ways, and when we do that, we can let God worry about whether our particular efforts "change the world." Fortunately, there are enough different types of Christians with unique gifts and interests to champion a Christian worldview in the public square, to combat global injustice, to minister to the poor, to build charitable organizations to relieve famine or disease, to make culture, and to fulfill a host of other redemptive tasks. Gabe Lyons describes Christians as "restorers" who, like a builder remodeling a beautiful but dilapidated mansion, are engaged in making the world what God intended it to be. He writes, "Instead of waiting for God to unveil the new heaven and the new earth, the rest of us can give the world a taste of what God's kingdom is all about—building up, repairing brokenness, showing mercy, reinstating hope, and generally adding value. In this expanded model, everyone plays an essential role."

> *Just as a carpenter needs training to remodel the house, so Christians need education in the complex cultural tasks of modern society if they are to be effective restorers of God's creation.*

But just as a carpenter needs training to remodel the house, so Christians need education in the complex cultural tasks of modern society if they are to be effective restorers of God's creation. As we saw in the previous chapter, the effects of the Fall are often complex. The work of restoration, therefore, requires rigorous study and *intelligent* action. The benefit of historical perspective can help us perceive systemic evils such as Nazism. But if you were a German Christian in the 1940s, how would you go about *fixing* such an institutional evil or alleviating the plight of the Jews? Doing so is no simple task.

Similarly, a college education can help us become aware of the subtle and systemic effects of the Fall on human society. But recognizing that young people in suburban Chicago graduate from high school at a higher rate than young people in inner-city Detroit is one thing; *changing* it is another. It requires an understanding of sociology and how social structures change, as well as politics, economics, and psychology. It will also help to study history to learn from the attempts of social reformers in the past. It might also involve business entrepreneurs who provide new sorts of job opportunities. In all these ways, a Christian college education equips us to redeem parts of creation more intelligently and more effectively.

Understanding our broad redemptive calling, therefore, makes college come alive in a whole new way. A major in engineering doesn't just prepare you for a career and a decent salary (though if you do your work well, that is a probable byproduct). It equips you to advance the work of restoration as an engineer—perhaps by developing clean-water technology that counteracts the effects of the Fall on our natural resources. A course in microeconomics doesn't just prepare you for a future job in business; it's one small part of the "engine" that will drive you into parts of the world that require an understanding of economic behavior in order to improve them. A law degree may equip you to advance justice in one corner of God's kingdom; or, as it did for Bryan Stevenson, it might pave the way to reform a flawed prison system. If we trace the connections, we can find all sorts of ways our college studies prepare us to contribute to God's redemptive work in the world.

Intelligent Evangelism

One more important way Christians advance Christ's reign in creation is by sharing the gospel verbally. As a *Christianity Today* editorial once put it, the world's greatest social need is for people to be reconciled to God spiritually. In a world in which millions of people do not believe in Christ, evangelism remains one of the Christian's redemptive tasks. I have waited to raise this point, however, because historically, evangelical Christians have been quick to focus on proclaiming the gospel, often to the exclusion of other concerns. When that happens, evangelism becomes forced, artificial, and unconvincing. But when Christians are actively and effectively engaged in the task of restoration in all parts of culture, the conditions are favorable for evangelism. Theologian Lesslie Newbigin observed, "Where the church is faithful to the Lord, *there* the powers of the Kingdom are present and people begin to ask the questions to which the Gospel is the answer."

To put it another way, we as Christians are called to excellence in our personal lives, in our careers, and in every other area of life. When we do that, the merits of Christianity are more likely to emerge naturally. Charles Murray once observed concerning the great Christian composer J. S. Bach, "When human beings are functioning at the heights of human capacity, it is a good idea to begin by assuming that they are doing something right. Johann Sebastian Bach does not need to explain himself; the beauty and excellence of his music itself make a case that his way of looking at the universe needs to be taken seriously." That doesn't mean one's vocation is simply a platform for evangelism, as if the only purpose for writing great music is to witness to other musicians. Such an argument would undermine the whole notion that our work as Christians is valuable in its own right. When verbal proclamation is appropriate, however, Christians need to do it intelligently. That's because for most of us who graduate from college, communicating the Christian story will occur in the course of our lives as professionals among society's educated class.

When I was a Christian-college student, I took a course entitled Personal Evangelism. In it we learned evangelistic techniques such as the Romans Road, in which the Christian led the nonbeliever through a series of passages in the New Testament book of Romans. That method depended on a big assumption—that the person being evangelized shares my belief that the Bible is the Word of God and speaks with authority about spiritual matters. However, a paradigm shift concerning the notion of truth has occurred in recent decades. For many modern Americans, what constitutes "truth" is defined individually or in communities; thus, multiple versions of truth can exist with little impact on each other. Moreover, the typical American would likely view Christianity as simply one of many ways of getting in touch with spiritual forces. What good does it do, therefore, for a Christian to simply quote the Bible, if most Americans view the Bible as just one of many inspiring books, along with the Koran and the Book of Mormon?

Effective evangelism requires that we understand the assumptions that lie beneath the thinking of modern secular people and the kinds of questions they are asking. You may have to discuss the nature of truth and the problem of evil with your coworker before you can get to the Bible. Perhaps you begin with a discussion at the lunch table of the theological implications of a recent film or book. For such conversations, a Christian college education can be valuable. You will learn logic and basic principles of evidence in a philosophy course; how the modern worldview has been shaped in world civilization; how to communicate persuasively in composition or oral communication; how to understand and empathize with the modern mentality as expressed in modern art and music; and how the Bible speaks to the modern condition in theology class. In short, We can think of our work of redemption as "broadcasting Mozart" into a fallen world.

> *We can think of our work of redemption as "broadcasting Mozart" into a fallen world.*

It's difficult to sum up such a vast and complex topic as Christian redemption, but perhaps a classic film will help: In *The Shawshank Redemption*, a wealthy businessman, played by Tim Robbins, has been wrongfully convicted of a crime and finds himself in the Massachusetts state penitentiary. The prison is controlled by a corrupt warden and his henchmen, who abuse the prisoners and siphon funds meant for the convicts into their own pockets. Because of his business skills, Robbins is chosen to work in the prison's main office. One day he is filing old musical albums and comes across a recording of Mozart's opera *The Marriage of Figaro*. Robbins's eyes light up as he gets an idea. He locks himself in the office, places the record on the record player, and broadcasts the music through the public address speakers across the entire prison grounds. As the camera pans across the prison yard, we see the dirty, demoralized prisoners momentarily entranced by the beauty of Mozart's aria flowing through the air. Recounts Morgan Freeman, Robbins's fellow prisoner, "I have no idea to this day what those two Italian ladies were singing about. . . . It was like some beautiful bird flapped into our drab cage and made those walls dissolve away. And for the briefest of moments, every last man at Shawshank felt free."

We can think of our work of redemption as "broadcasting Mozart" into a fallen world. Our college education prepares us for a vocation that will help infuse truth, love, beauty, and order into a world that is marred by injustice, ugliness, and disorder. But we can carry the analogy further. Tim Robbins was powerless to change the prison system. A prison revolt inspired by a Mozart aria would have been good drama but not very realistic. Eventually, the prison guards break into Robbins's office, destroy the Mozart record, and throw him into solitary confinement, and the prison reverts to the status quo. Thus, Robbins's contribution was to make the conditions more bearable for his fellow prisoners and to point them to a better world beyond the prison walls.

But if Robbins had wielded more power in the penitentiary—for example, as a prison guard, or even as the warden—then merely providing beautiful music for the prisoners would have been inadequate.

We would expect him to work to correct the abuses and injustices of the prison complex. Money intended for the penitentiary would purchase new clothes for the prisoners, not supplement the warden's private bank account. Guards who abused prisoners would be punished. Prisoners would be rehabilitated, not just punished for their crimes. Robbins's "redemptive" work would have changed significantly if his cultural position had been different.

As Christians, therefore, we need to have the wisdom to discern at what points in our culture we have the power, and the duty, to change the system itself. For some, our main redemptive calling may be to use our careers and talents to "broadcast Mozart" into the world and to evangelize those within the system—to exercise Hunter's "faithful presence" in our particular sphere of creation. Others will be called to change the system itself—to practice, like Bryan Stevenson, a "faithful resistance" to the status quo. Often, of course, it will be a combination of both. In each case, a Christian college education is valuable. It not only prepares us for a career, but more importantly, it equips us to play our role in restoring God's creation to the way it was supposed to be.

A Note on Sources

The concept of *shalom* is discussed in Cornelius Plantinga, *Engaging God's World* (Grand Rapids: Eerdmans, 2002), 14–15. Wolters's D-Day analogy and the sacred/secular diagram are found in Albert Wolter, *Creation Regained* (Grand Rapids: Eerdmans, 1985), 66–70. Richard Mouw is quoted in Andy Crouch, *Making Culture* (Downers Grove, IL: InterVarsity Press, 2008), 163–74. Lyons's remark about "restorers" is in Gabe Lyons, *The Next Christians* (New York: Doubleday, 2010), 60. Lesslie Newbigin is quoted in Lyons, 195. Charles Murray's remark concerning J. S. Bach is from "For God's Eye: The Surprising Role of Christianity in Cultural Achievement," in *The American Enterprise* (October/November, 2003). The *Christianity Today* editorial "The Greatest Social Need" was published in January 2009.

In addition to the sources cited above, two important works on Christians' cultural calling are Charles Colson, *How Shall We Now Live* (Carol Stream, IL: Tyndale House, 1999) and James Davison Hunter, *To Change the World* (Oxford: Oxford University Press, 2010). A vivid example of redemption in one corner of creation mentioned in this chapter is Bryan Stevenson, *Just Mercy: A Story of Justice and Redemption* (New York: Spiegel and Grau, 2014).

Questions for Reflection and Discussion

1. How would your particular community function differently if *shalom* were more present there?

2. Why do you think Christ has allowed so much time to pass between his first coming and his second coming?

3. What is one way that your own particular course of study stands in need of redemption?

4. Do you anticipate your particular calling in life to be "broadcasting Mozart" into the prison, or changing the prison system itself? Explain.

5. How would you approach college differently if you envisioned it as preparation for a life of reconciliation and restoration?

6. What is a recent book or film you have encountered that would enable you to more effectively communicate the Christian story to a non-Christian?

6 INTEGRATING FAITH AND LEARNING

A Basic Introduction

THE preceding chapters summarized the basic elements of the Christian story—Creation, Fall, and Redemption—and described some ways that they relate to a Christian college. But what does all this have to do with the actual academic process? Isn't algebra simply algebra, whether one is a Christian or not? It's time to explore more specifically how Christianity relates to the nuts and bolts of coursework at a Christian college, using a term that you'll probably encounter often: *integration*. This chapter will explain what Christian educators call the "integration of faith and learning" and then lay out some ways Christians attempt to connect their Christian faith to their particular disciplines.

We'll begin, however, by identifying some common misconceptions of what it means to integrate faith and learning. First, integration is not simply a matter of warm personal relationships between professors and students. I once attended a faculty seminar on integration in which one professor described his pride at seeing a colleague hug each of her students when they received their diplomas at graduation. He concluded, "If that's not the integration of faith and learning, I don't know what is." Actually, it's not. While of course the nurturing of meaningful relationships between professors and students is a good thing (and one of the most valuable features of a Christian college), it is not what we typically mean by the integration of faith and learning. Such mentoring relationships can and do occur at secular and Christian institutions alike.

More than just denoting the relationship between professor and student, the integration of faith and learning concerns the actual classroom environment itself. Some Christians have interpreted that statement to mean that integrating faith and learning is synonymous with praying before class. Of course, opening class with prayer is generally a good thing (students especially appreciate it on examination days), but that's not what is meant by integration. If nothing in the professor's approach to the subject has anything to do with his or her Christian faith after the opening prayer, then a real, substantive integration of faith and learning has not occurred. The opening prayer may simply serve as a convenient tool to focus students' minds on the subject and remind them of their overall purpose in college.

This notion, that integration of faith and learning is primarily a matter of setting a spiritual atmosphere, stems from a shallow understanding of the relationship between Christian faith and academic inquiry. Some Christian educators have seemed to function as if Christianity and secular learning inhabit separate spheres. We learn spiritual and moral truths from the Bible, some would claim, and we learn about the physical world from academic disciplines. Thus, the task of a Christian college is to cultivate a pious atmosphere outside of class (through chapel, prayer groups, weekend retreats, and the like) while encouraging rigorous academic inquiry in the classroom.

The problem with the "separate spheres" approach to learning is that it overlooks the fact that much of what we learn from science, psychology, and other disciplines has theological and moral implications. Furthermore, while not an academic textbook, the Bible nevertheless contains many implications about the makeup of the universe, the events and meaning of history, human nature, and other academic questions. To cite just one obvious example, the Christian who believes the biblical account of Jesus's bodily resurrection would, by necessity, *dis*believe an archaeologist's claim to have discovered the bones of Jesus of Nazareth in an ancient Palestinian tomb.

The integration of faith and learning, therefore, goes beyond a pious atmosphere to the academic discipline itself. But even here, the concept can be misunderstood. Some Christians interpret integration primarily as a matter of including religious topics within one's area of study. I once attended a lecture by an English professor who explained that when teaching poetry, she used passages from the Psalms as examples of various meters. That's fine, but it's not integration. We would not claim that a Christian carpenter who uses a Bible to prop up a table leg is integrating Christianity and furniture-making. Likewise, professors who insert religious material into their classes are not necessarily integrating faith and learning. Perceiving integration to be primarily a matter of studying "religious" topics allows professors in, say, biology, to delegate the integration of faith and learning to those in theology while they concentrate on doing "real" science.

So if inadequate notions of the integration of faith and learning abound, what do we really mean by the term? To fully understand integration, we need to refer back to the introductory chapter on Christian worldview. Simply put, integrating faith and learning means relating one's Christian worldview to an academic discipline. It is the ongoing process of understanding a subject in all its complexity in relation to the Christian, and then living out its moral and cultural implications. As such, integration involves not just an opening prayer but the class session; and it applies to biology class as well as to Bible class. Scores of books have been written on this subject, but for our purposes we can boil down the integration of faith and learning as operating on three basic levels.

> *Simply put, integrating faith and learning means relating one's Christian worldview to an academic discipline.*

The Motivational–Relational Level

The first level draws on some of our observations in the previous chapters: our Christian faith motivates us to learn and to apply a positive attitude toward any subject of study as a way to grow in our relationship with God. This is integration at its most basic, but it's probably the most common level for the college student. For many non-Christians, the purpose of college is quite simple—to perform well, get good grades, and build an impressive resume for a career. In light of Creation, Fall, and Redemption, however, it should be clear that Christians have a higher purpose and deeper motivation for going to class. Each subject provides an opportunity to know God better, to more fully bear his image, and to become better able to participate in God's redemptive activity in the world.

Let me illustrate my point concerning the doctrine of Creation: years ago, my son was cleaning out our garage and came across some old spiral notebooks lying in the bottom of a box. They were my journals from my college days. Naturally, he was keenly interested in reading through them and learning more about his father during his developmental years—though I was more ambivalent about the prospect of my son reading my college journals. Imagine, however, that I had hired my neighbor's son to clean out the garage. He may have been amused at an adult's college journals lying around in a garage, but he probably would have had little interest in reading through them.

> *Our Christian faith motivates us to learn and to apply a positive attitude toward any subject of study as a way to grow in our relationship with God. This is integration at its most basic.*

My son's interest in the journals stemmed from his relationship to me. I'm his father, and the journals reveal things about his father that he wouldn't otherwise know. In the same way, the doctrine of Creation means that the universe is

God's journal, which reveals things about him that we would not learn in any other way. It's what theologians call God's "general revelation" or the "book of nature," which expresses his characteristics and qualities as distinct from the "special revelation" of the Bible.

Our basic motivation for learning biology, for example, stems from our relationship to God as the Creator of the wonderfully complex life forms we study. Moreover, the doctrine of the *imago dei* implies that God instills in each of us a natural curiosity about his creation, which we express when we study cells, algebra, or the French Revolution. And if that's not enough motivation, there's also the doctrine of redemption, which implies that fixing this broken world begins by more deeply understanding the problems facing it. Integrating a Christian worldview and academics, therefore, begins with applying a positive attitude toward learning as rooted in our Christian identity.

Such rhetoric may sound good in theory, but it's more difficult to apply at the ground level. Having taught Survey of Western Civilization at 7:30 A.M., I can attest that my students know all too well that going to class does not always seem like reading the journals of God. So here are a few practical suggestions. First, if your instructor doesn't open class with prayer, it may be helpful to say a silent prayer as a way to remind yourself of the larger purpose of class. It could be something as basic as the prayer "For Education," adapted from the *Book of Common Prayer*: "Almighty God, the fountain of all wisdom: Enlighten by your Holy Spirit those who teach and those who learn, that rejoicing in the knowledge of your truth, we may worship you and serve you better." Or one could pray at the beginning of class, "God, what is it in *this class* today that will enable me to know you better and love you more?" Such prayers serve to remind us that God is ultimately the source of truth and that every subject can help us better worship and glorify him.

Second, work with other students to gain interest in and understanding of the subject. When I was in college, I enjoyed literature but was not particularly fond of chemistry. I had fellow students, however, who could get excited about learning chemistry. Discussing chemistry with them helped me not only understand the subject better; I also came to appreciate how the study of chemistry actually deepened their relationship with God. Thus, it enabled me to have a more positive attitude toward the subject. Discussing course materials with others outside of class—during lunch or in the dormitory, for example—can increase your understanding and appreciation of the subject, even if it's outside your natural area of interest.

There is also value in discussing course material directly with your professor. While doing so may seem intimidating (at least it was for introverts like myself), keep in mind that the typical Christian college professor chooses to teach at a Christian institution so that he or she can personally interact with students, not just write books and do research. Visiting professors during office hours and seeing their love for a subject not only can spark your own interest in the subject, but it can foster the sort of mentoring relationships that are at the heart of a Christian college experience. Personally, I can trace my interest in becoming a professional academic back to a handwritten note that I received from my Old Testament professor in Bible college.

The Intellectual–Foundational Level

Most Christians would acknowledge that Christian faith should result in a positive motivation toward learning. The integration of faith and learning, however, occurs not just at the attitudinal level but at the intellectual level as well. As explained in the introductory chapter, all academic inquiry stems from certain assumptions about the nature of reality, God's existence, human nature, and so on. Integrating faith and learning means that we intentionally connect our Christian worldview to the area of study. What does psychology look like, for example, to the Christian psychologist who believes human beings are not simply randomly evolved organisms but creatures with souls made in God's image? A course in psychology that integrates faith and learning at the intellectual level will tease out such implications of a Christian view of human nature.

> *The more that a discipline deals with the nature of human beings, their cultural products, and the nature of ultimate reality, however, the more explicitly worldview assumptions influence the discourse.*

But back to the chapter's opening question: Is there a "Christian" algebra? Not necessarily. When it comes to applying a Christian worldview at the intellectual-foundational level, some disciplines will tend to integrate faith and learning more explicitly than others. There are fewer areas in mathematics where a Christian worldview about the nuts and bolts of the subject is distinctive from a secular worldview than in, say, philosophy, a subject in which one's assumptions about the nature of reality are critical. We can thus think of integration as a continuum. Disciplines such as physics and chemistry focus almost exclusively on physical matter, and worldview questions do not typically intrude on the subject. When doing their jobs as chemists, Christians, atheists, Muslims, and others will generally agree about the makeup of molecules and their interactions, despite their different worldviews. Christian scholars may bring different motivations to their disciplines and reach different ethical conclusions than others do, but in the actual scholarship itself, Christian faith will likely be more *implicit* than explicit.

The more a discipline deals with the nature of human beings, their cultural products, and the nature of ultimate reality, however, the more explicitly worldview assumptions influence the discourse, since these are questions over which Christians and non-Christians are more likely to disagree. In psychology, for instance, one is never very far from basic worldview questions, such as, "Do human beings have a soul?" and "What is the basis of human motivation?" As we move from mathematics and natural science to the social sciences and the humanities, the more explicit one's worldview becomes, and thus more opportunity will exist for the integration of faith and learning, as the following diagram illustrates.

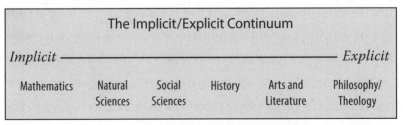

The Implicit/Explicit Continuum

Implicit ————————————————————— *Explicit*

| Mathematics | Natural Sciences | Social Sciences | History | Arts and Literature | Philosophy/ Theology |

Fig. 6.1. The Implicit–Explicit Continuum

Even in the areas toward the left side of the continuum, however, the opportunity for integration at the intellectual-foundational level never completely disappears. For example, in mathematics, scholars may differ over such foundational questions as, "Are numbers real or imagined?" "Is mathematical truth 'out there' to be discovered, or is it invented in the mind of the mathematician?" The answers to these questions are inescapably linked to one's worldview. In the 1930s, Nazi scholars argued that there was a "German" mathematics and a "German" physics, as distinct from "Jewish" mathematics or physics; they thought mathematical and physical truth was not "out there" to be discovered but subject to the perspectives of one's race. Their assumptions about race and culture impacted their understanding even of the so-called "hard" sciences.

The opportunity to ask deeper questions about our disciplines may lie just beneath the surface, if we allow our Christian beliefs to operate fully. No one exemplifies this truth better than David Smith, a German language professor at Calvin University and an expert on Christian pedagogy. Language textbooks, of course, typically use situations from daily life to teach students grammar and new vocabulary. While using a standard textbook, Dr. Smith noticed that the daily life situations used by German textbooks consisted mainly of things such as shopping, going on vacation, going out to restaurants with friends, attending concerts and other events, and working out. The implicit message of such textbooks was the communication of a notion of the good life—consuming things, enjoying life, and seeking self-fulfillment—that was different from a Christian understanding of the good life. Experiences such as ministering to the poor, denying one's own material desires, worshipping, and death were conspicuously absent. Smith thus sought to construct a language textbook that would express a different story about the meaning of life. The point that Smith makes is not that secular textbooks are bad and should not be used. Rather, it's that Christians need to dig beneath the surface and ask deeper questions about the stories their disciplines are telling about the nature of reality.

A few years ago, some psychologists made headlines when they conducted what became known as the "invisible gorilla" experiment. They showed viewers a short video in which a group of people passed basketballs around, and they asked the viewers to count the number of passes made by the people in the white shirts. In the middle of the video, a man in a gorilla suit strolls into the middle of the action, faces the camera and thumps his chest, and then leaves. Amazingly, half the viewers never saw the gorilla (including me, the first time I watched it). The experiment vividly demonstrated an important truth: humans have a remarkable ability to see what they are looking for and not see what they don't look for. Often what scholars "see" in the data is shaped by their worldview assumptions and the questions they bring to their scholarship. Integrating faith and learning at the intellectual-foundational level, therefore, means allowing our Christian beliefs to raise provocative questions about our disciplines and, like David Smith's critique of the German textbook, seeing assumptions in our disciplines that others may overlook.

The Applied–Ethical Level

One of the potential dangers of a worldview approach to integration is that it can be misconstrued to imply that once we as Christians have "figured out" a discipline or critiqued it intellectually, our task is done. Christianity, however, is not a philosophy; it's a way of thinking *and acting* in the world. As cultural beings, our encounter with any new information or technique will ultimately prompt us to ask what use it will have in our actual lives. Karl Marx famously declared, "Up to now the purpose of philosophy has been to understand the world. But the purpose of philosophy is to *change* the world." As Christians, we do not have to accept all of Marx's philosophy to agree with him that as agents of redemption in the world, we should seek to understand what difference a subject makes to the world around us.

> *The final way of integrating faith and learning . . . involves applying the knowledge from a particular discipline to the world in a way that furthers God's creative or redemptive purposes.*

The final way of integrating faith and learning, therefore, involves applying the knowledge from a particular discipline to the world in a way that furthers God's creative or redemptive purposes. Psychology can be used to *help* people, not just to understand them. Obviously, that involves doing, not just thinking. When one moves from the subject itself to the *application* of that knowledge, however, one often encounters a host of ethical questions that cannot be answered apart from worldviews. Einstein's famous equation $e=mc^2$, for example, sparks little debate between Christian and non-Christian scholars. However, when one applies this scientific insight to society in terms of nuclear energy, all sorts of controversial questions arise. Should we develop nuclear bombs? If so, should they ever be used? What about nuclear power plants, which provide more energy with less pollution than fossil fuels, but which also may pose a greater long-term threat to society and the environment?

The same can be said for a seemingly "hard" discipline such as engineering. For example, engineers and builders may generally agree that a thinner, lighter window material could save thousands of dollars in material costs when constructing high-rise buildings. However, the cheaper windows may be more likely to blow out during a storm, endangering pedestrians below. At what point does using lower-cost windows that increase the risk of human injury become immoral? The answer to this question depends on the relative value one places on human beings and therefore on human safety—in other words, on worldview questions.

Here's a particularly relevant example in the seemingly objective discipline of health care: During a global pandemic, how far should governments go in curtailing civil liberties and disrupting the economy in order to protect human life? How does one balance the competing interests of public health, personal freedom, and economic well-being? Integrating faith and learning involves going from a subject itself to working out its practical and ethical consequences for individuals and cultures. And this is why capstone ethics courses abound at Christian colleges—courses such as bio-ethics, business ethics, and medical ethics, and the like.

Asking the Integrative Question

This discussion raises an important point. Wherever one's discipline falls on the continuum, one of the best ways to go about the actual task of integrating faith and learning is to ask what Christian scholar Harold Heie calls the "integrative question"—that is, a question that cannot be answered without reference to both the discipline itself and Christian faith. Examples of such questions abound, and often what brings a subject alive to Christian college students is developing and wrestling with these sorts of questions. Here are just a few examples from across the implicit–explicit continuum:

> *Natural Science:* Can human consciousness and rationality be explained completely in evolutionary terms? Concerning the origins of the universe, can science explain the Big Bang, or does this event point beyond itself to causes outside the bounds of science?

> *Political Science:* Is representative democracy the most "Christian" form of government possible? If so, then how far should one go to create such a system in nondemocratic nations? Is a "war for democracy" worth the cost?

> *Journalism:* At what point does the journalist's obligation to uncover the truth of a story conflict with the need to respect the privacy of vulnerable human beings who are made in God's image? How does one balance commitment to the truth with respect and compassion for others?

> *Economics:* Is a tax system that takes money from the wealthy to distribute to the poor a proper application of biblical social

ethics, or is it an infringement on the Christian notion of human freedom? Should governments regulate the economy merely to ensure a level playing field, or to achieve greater economic equality?

Computer Science: To what extent is a programmer responsible for considering how a program will be used in real people's lives over time? How does an Internet company balance the power of search engine analytics with the value of human privacy?

Literature: To what extent are we obligated to read a text according to the author's original purpose? Is it possible to transcend the bounds of race, class, gender, and culture and truly understand an author's intent? In other words, is there anything truly universal in Shakespeare?

Music and Art: Is beauty simply in the eye of the beholder, or are there external, objective standards of beauty that can be applied to all works of art? Does the eight-note major scale sound "right" to us simply because we have been conditioned that way, or does it correspond to some universal standard created by God? Are some art forms more "Christian" than others?

Questions such as these abound in every discipline, and their value is that they challenge us not only to know our discipline, but to think more deeply about our Christian faith and its implications for the world around us. Integrative questions also lead to another observation: the integration of faith and learning continues *throughout* one's life as a Christian learner. One does not "get" integration in an introductory college class and then go on to other topics in one's subject. Remember the crossword puzzle metaphor in the opening chapter? Because our Christian worldview is dynamic, not static, integration is a two-way street. That is, our Christian worldview affects the subject we study, but the truth learned in that subject may in turn influence our Christian worldview. This back-and-forth process continues throughout our lives as Christian learners.

Here's an example in history. As a Christian historian, I have been interested in the history of American slavery, and my Christian worldview affects my understanding of the topic in a variety of ways. In the first place, as a historian, I can discover causes and effects in history because God has ordered the universe in a rational, cause-and-effect manner. There's some sense of basic order to history. Moreover, the lives of individual slaves are worth studying because they are human beings made in God's image. Also, one can expect to find evidence that religion played an important role in the slaves' lives because as creatures made in God's image, human beings are inherently religious. These are all assumptions I bring to my study of history because of my Christian faith.

My study of slavery, however, also impacts my Christian worldview. For example, many slaves were devout Christians. Thus, one thing the history of slavery reveals is that for some reason, God may allow his followers to spend their entire lives under oppression and engaged in seemingly meaningless tasks. Such a conclusion challenges my modern American middle-class assumption that Christians who are "in God's will" should naturally have fulfilling lives and careers. Also, this basic fact—that the slave communities were generally Christian—leads me to question the conventional Christian belief that America has represented "God's country" throughout much of its history. In fact, the study of slavery suggests that nineteenth-century America may have more closely resembled a New Egypt enslaving God's chosen people than it did a New Israel. It may motivate me as a Christian to better recognize the racial injustice that has existed throughout American history and work to promote racial justice. As the study of history illustrates, this dialectical process of adjustment and readjustment between what we believe as Christians and what we learn as scholars continues throughout our lives.

In closing, let me offer a word of caution: consciously integrating faith and learning by asking the "big questions" will not always comprise the majority of a course at the Christian college, nor should it. We should ask the big questions of all subjects, but much of our time will be spent on the more mundane level of doing basic scholarship in the discipline. Looking back on my college basketball days, my most vivid memories are of playing intense games against rival teams, especially those games in the national tournament. But measured in terms of actual time spent,

> *Our Christian worldview affects the subject we study, but the truth learned in that subject may in turn influence our Christian worldview. This back-and-forth process continues throughout our lives as Christian learners.*

those particular experiences were not the norm. As any athlete knows, most of my actual time playing basketball was spent doing drills, practicing plays, working on fundamentals, and worst of all, running sprints. The countless hours engaged in such activities provided the foundation for those games I remember so vividly.

The application to academics is obvious. Asking the big questions in a particular discipline is only possible if one understands the subject in the first place. A class on calculus will not get very far if students constantly interrupt the professor to ask, "Are logarithms discovered or invented?" While such questions are important, they should not prevent us from doing the hard work of understanding the details of the subject itself. It does little good to debate the significance of cell structures to the theory of evolution if one doesn't understand how mitochondria function in the first place. Integrating faith and learning in biology is not a substitute for the important task of memorizing the stages of mitosis.

Hence, the calling of the Christian in college is not very different from the Christian life in general. Our big tasks as Christians, such as redeeming creation, usually manifest themselves in simple faithfulness to seemingly mundane tasks like showing up for work on time and serving one's neighbor. In the same way, the lofty calling of a Christian college student—understanding God's creation and becoming an agent of redemption in the world—generally works itself out in simple ways such as going to class and faithfully pursuing one's calling as a Christian learner.

A Note on Sources

The integration of faith and learning has become a widely discussed subject at Christian colleges and among Christian scholars. Thus, books and articles on the subject abound—one bibliography on the subject lists 348 volumes. For this brief introduction, I have drawn from several sources, most notably David I. Smith and James K. A. Smith, *Teaching and Christian Practices: Reshaping Faith and Learning* (Grand Rapids: Eerdmans, 2011); Perry Glanzer and Nathan Alleman, *The Outrageous Idea of Christian Teaching* (Oxford: Oxford University Press, 2019); David Smith, *On Christian Teaching: Practicing Faith in the Classroom* (Grand Rapids: Eerdmans, 2018); and a classic, Arthur Holmes, *The Idea of a Christian College* (Grand Rapids: Eerdmans, 1996).

The discussion of the Implicit–Explicit Continuum is drawn from C. Stephen Evans, "The Calling of the Christian Scholar-Teacher," in Douglas Henry and Bob Agee, eds., *Faithful Learning and the Christian Scholarly Vocation* (Grand Rapids: Eerdmans, 2003), 26–49, and from Douglas and Rhonda Jacobsen, eds., *Scholarship and Christian Faith: Enlarging the Conversation* (Oxford: Oxford University Press, 2004). Heie's notion of the integrative question can be found in Harry Lee Poe, *Christianity in the Academy* (Ada, MI: Baker Academic, 2004), 158–60.

Questions for Reflection and Discussion

1. Have you encountered any of the mistaken views of integration in your academic career?

2. Why do some subjects lend themselves to integration more explicitly than other subjects?

3. What is an example of an "integrative question" in your major field of study?

4. Why would a course at a Christian college not necessarily spend most of its time consciously integrating faith and learning?

5. Do you think it would be better to emphasize the integration of faith and learning in a freshman-level course or in a senior-level course? Why?

PART THREE

Making the Most of College

7   AN EDUCATION THAT LASTS

Thinking Creatively and Globally

IMAGINE the following scenario. You aspire to compete in the Olympics. You arrange your lifestyle so you can compete as a world-class athlete—you get plenty of sleep, carefully monitor your diet, and of course spend hours a day in training and preparation. But here's the catch: the Olympic organizers have decided that it would be fun to change the Olympic events every four years, and to keep the events a secret until just before the games begin. How would you prepare for the Olympics? Naturally, you would focus on activities that make you as flexible and adaptable as possible. Weight training would be crucial, but you wouldn't want to bulk up like a Russian weight lifter because you might be required to run a hundred-meter dash. It would be important to develop your hand-eye coordination for table tennis, but also hone your footwork in case you were called on to do the triple jump.

While such a scenario may be far-fetched in athletics, it's not very far from the world that college students enter upon graduation. As Thomas Friedman noted in his classic work *The World Is Flat*, in today's globalized, decentralized, and rapidly changing world, preparing for the future is like "training for the Olympics without knowing which sport you will compete in." What kind of college education best prepares students for such a world? Actually, it's the kind of education that most Christian colleges provide: a liberal arts–based, globally oriented education.

That last sentence will need some unpacking. The previous chapters have focused on the *Christian* dimensions of education by exploring the Christian story and the integration of faith and learning. But most Christian colleges also describe their educational program in terms of the liberal arts. While educators like to throw the "liberal arts" phrase around, few people outside of academia know what the term means or why it is used. This chapter, therefore, will discuss the nature of a liberal arts education and explain why a broad education that goes beyond career preparation is so valuable in today's society.

First, a little history: the liberal arts as an educational program emerged about 2,500 years ago in ancient Greece. In democratic Athens, the free citizen was expected to be able to speak persuasively and eloquently in a public forum. Thus a "liberal arts" education in the classical world focused on grammar—for the study of texts—and rhetoric, or the art of persuasive speech. With the rise of Christianity in the late Roman Empire, the liberal arts became grafted onto the needs of Christian education, namely biblical interpretation, the study of theology, and the nurture of personal piety. Medieval Christian universities expanded the subjects of the liberal arts to include not only grammar, rhetoric, and logic but also math, music, and astronomy.

During the Protestant Reformation of the 1500s, reformers like Martin Luther and John Calvin developed a system of education that combined Christian instruction and classical learning. It was designed to produce what they called a "wise and eloquent piety." As we have seen, such a curriculum became the norm at early American colleges like Harvard and Yale. The rise of modern science to pre-eminence in the 1800s, however, challenged this traditional liberal arts program, and universities changed in two ways. First, the liberal arts were expanded to include natural and social sciences such as biology and psychology. Second, colleges allowed students to select a specialized course of study, called a major, that would prepare them for a particular career. In most cases, however, specialized majors did not simply replace the liberal arts. Rather, the two curricula were combined into a four-year under-graduate program.

A liberal arts course seeks to connect the nonspecialist to a historical conversation about some of the big questions in life that have been ongoing within a particular discipline.

Thus, most Christian colleges today combine study in a major with a liberal arts core, which they call "general education" or "core curriculum." So what makes something a "core" class? First, a liberal arts course seeks to connect the nonspecialist to a historical conversation about some of the big questions in life that have been ongoing within a particular discipline. For example, a core class in introductory biology will not only cover the five phases of mitosis but also explore the big questions in the discipline, such as, What is life? Where did it come from? What is unique about humans? And of course, at a Christian college such a course will challenge students to integrate a Christian worldview with such questions. To put it in the terms of the previous chapter, a Christian core class will deal with integrative questions, not just technical questions.

Second, a liberal arts course generally seeks to impact who we *are* rather than what we do. It develops internal qualities such as depth of insight, clarity of understanding, appreciation for cultural activity, communication skill, and moral commitment. Again, an analogy from sports may be helpful. As a basketball player, I can benefit both from practicing my free-throw technique and from lifting weights. Practicing free throws improves a particular skill that I need in a basketball game. Weight training benefits me indirectly in basketball but also in other sports as well, because it changes who I am (in this case, my muscle mass) and doesn't just hone a skill. We can think of major courses as free-throw training, providing specific knowledge or skills that are needed for a particular "game." Core classes, by contrast, are more like weight training. They develop who we are at a more fundamental level. Thus, they prepare us for a wider variety of activities, but also like weight training, their practical value may not be as immediately apparent as a specific course in a major.

So why are the liberal arts still important today? To answer that question, let's look more closely at two important features of the world college graduates are entering. First, we inhabit a world that is growing simultaneously more technological and more in need of big-picture, creative thinkers. The previous century was known as the Information Age, in which knowledge and information fueled the economies of advanced nations. Professions developed, and a new social class, the white-collar class, came to dominate society. The most advanced societies consisted of knowledge workers who produced and processed information. For example, factories that produced automobiles could be moved to Mexico where labor costs were cheaper, but the managers needed to plan, develop, and distribute the cars remained in their offices in Detroit. In such a world, the desirable traits of college graduates were left-brained traits such as linear thinking and logical analysis. Law, computer programming, and engineering were the seemingly safe professions that would always provide job security and a good paycheck.

The twenty-first century, however, has witnessed a transformation. Advances in technology and communications, most notably the Internet, mean that even complex tasks can be automated and outsourced to other locations. Twenty years ago, you would have paid an accountant to prepare your taxes. Now you can purchase a login ID for TurboTax to perform the same function. In the Information Age, a law degree seemingly guaranteed the graduate lifetime job security and a good income. Today, however, the Internet is breaking through the information monopoly that

Just as machines replaced human power to dig coal shafts in the 1800s, new technologies and global communications today are providing the capacity to replace the knowledge workers of the twentieth century.

has long been the source of security to lawyers. Need a divorce? CompleteCase.com will handle it for a few hundred dollars. In other words, just as machines replaced human power to dig coal shafts in the 1800s, new technologies and global communications today are providing the capacity to replace the knowledge workers of the twentieth century.

Thus we have entered what scholars call the Conceptual Age, one in which creators, designers, and collaborators command the highest value. The right brain—the part that synthesizes information, sees the big picture, envisions new scenarios, and empathizes with others—is as essential to the modern economy as the left brain. Writing code for an iPhone is one thing; but it takes a different sort of mind to envision the need for and value of an iPhone in the first place, and to design one that has that mysterious quality of "feeling right" to the user. Creativity, not just computation, is the important trait of the future.

All this has been described well by Scott Hartley in his book *The Fuzzy and the Techie: Why the Liberal Arts Will Rule the Digital World.* In the increasingly technological world that we inhabit, Hartley observes, "soft" skills such as complex thinking, social competence, collaboration, and creative problem solving are increasingly valuable. Moreover, advances in technology are making its applications increasingly accessible to nontechies. The building of a website, for example, used to require the services of a computer programmer. Now you just download Squarespace or Wix and do it yourself. Hartley concludes, "The fuzzy combined with the techie is the formula for the most transformative and successful innovations—the ones that will most effectively solve the many vexing problems to be tackled and will most humanely enhance our lives."

There's another important feature of the modern world. The programmer writing code for the iPhone—or the technician fielding your phone call when your computer screen freezes up—may be just as likely to be working in a converted warehouse in Asia as in Silicon Valley. Such a fact points to another fundamental transformation described by Thomas Friedman in *The World Is Flat*. Advances in technology and communications have produced a "flat" world in which goods are produced through global supply chains, and workers in America compete with workers in Brazil and China. The typical corporation today is multinational. The concept for a car may originate in Detroit, but the design plans may be developed in Germany, the parts produced in Mexico, and the car assembled in Alabama. Furthermore, the rise of the Internet means that the free market can pinpoint the cheapest labor source, whether that is in sewing garments or writing computer code. Outsourcing affects not just factory workers but computer programmers.

A technological, rapidly changing global economy means that nations at the cutting edge of these changes such as the United States will increasingly find their niche in the soft skill areas described by Scott Hartley. Creative work will occupy a growing segment of the American economy. Of course, there will always be a need for people who can grow food, build structures, and work machines. But college graduates in America, regardless of their major, will typically be expected to do the creative work of research and development, designing new products and processes, and collaborating with workers in other cultures. And as many of us discovered as a result of the COVID-19 disruptions, collaboration by Zoom can occur effectively across cultures and time zones.

All of these social changes naturally have tremendous implications for colleges in the United States. Education for a "flat" world, Friedman notes, must focus on "teaching students how to learn, instilling passion and curiosity in them, and developing their intuitive skills." A generation ago, many Americans saw the value of a college education as primarily training a graduate in specific job skills. Today a college education has to prepare graduates to think creatively, work effectively with people from diverse cultures, and adapt quickly to technological and social changes. To return to our Olympics analogy—if Americans a generation ago went to college to prepare to be pole-vaulters, students today must prepare to be decathletes. Specifically, such a social transformation has three lessons for the Christian college student.

Don't Stress Out over a Major

In a world where technologies change rapidly and whole new economies can emerge on short notice, the particular major that one pursues as an undergraduate is less important than the overall qualities, knowledge base, and skills that one develops. Years ago, *USA Today* surveyed the undergraduate majors of chief executive officers of Fortune 500 companies. Surprisingly, only 15 percent of them had majored in business, and a large number of them majored in seemingly esoteric liberal arts disciplines such as philosophy, art history, or literature. In light of the social changes discussed above, that should not be surprising. A major such as philosophy develops the sort of critical reasoning and communication skills one would expect from a leader of a modern corporation.

That fact also subverts a common myth believed by many, especially since the 2009 recession, that engineering and business majors get good jobs while English majors become graduate students or baristas. Actually, the data consistently shows that while science and engineering majors tend to earn higher salaries right out of college, liberal arts majors catch up over time. Moreover, liberal arts majors are more likely to pursue a variety of jobs over their lifetime. That's why educators sometimes remark that a business major prepares you for your first job, while a history major prepares you for the job you'll have ten years from now.

When I was a professor, to alleviate "major stress" among my college freshmen, I would play a match game in which students attempted to match university officials with their major in college. To their surprise, students discovered that their college president was an English major, the vice president for student development was a psychology major, and the chief financial officer majored in, of all things, zoology. Of course, the student who wants to be an engineer will have to get started on an engineering degree right away. But for the vast majority of college students, the fluid, global work environment means that what one majors in is much less important than the broader skills and perspectives that a college education will provide. As one business executive remarked, "Everybody ten years out of college is doing something completely different from what they went to college for."

Furthermore, the skills one develops in supposedly impractical majors may bear fruit in unexpected ways, as I have discovered

> *For the vast majority of college students, the fluid, global work environment means that what one majors in is much less important than the broader skills and perspectives that a college education will provide.*

firsthand. I was a history major in college, mainly because I had no idea what I wanted to do in life and I liked reading stories about the past. In some ways, my history major directly impacted my career, since I went on to complete a PhD in history and become a professor. But after being a professor for five years, I went on to become a dean, a provost, an officer at a higher education association, and most recently a consultant in study abroad and online education.

So was my history major irrelevant to my current career? Hardly. What I learned as a historian was to wade through a mountain of historical facts, perceive the big picture amid the details, and communicate a reasonable, compelling story from the data. The numerous events that occurred in eastern North America in the 1770s and 1780s, for example, don't simply explain themselves. It takes a historian to select events, find a common thread, and tell the story of the American Revolution.

I no longer write history books, but like just about anyone engaged in white-collar work, I still interpret and communicate information. For example, one of my responsibilities as provost was to prepare updates on academics twice a year for the board of trustees. I would have a wealth of data at my disposal: student graduation rates, course evaluations, enrollment data by major, curricular changes, faculty professional activities, and more. But trustees don't want a pile of data; they want a *story* that explains what the current academic situation is and where it is going. My task was to sift through the facts, perceive the story the data was telling, and communicate that story in a compelling way to the trustees. I was an administrator functioning as a historian. Twenty years ago when I wrote a research paper on Japan during World War II, I had no idea I would use those same skills to write a trustee report.

Events of recent years have reinforced the basic truth that we cannot predict how society, much less our own careers, will change. The choice of a particular major, therefore, is less important than the transferable skills one learns both in a major and in other courses. That doesn't mean you should major in philosophy rather than computer science; it means you should feel free to follow your God-given interests and passions in your college years and not get hung up over the presumed practicality of a particular major. Which leads to the second lesson.

Take the Liberal Arts Core Seriously

One sometimes hears students refer to core curriculum courses as stuff to "get out of the way" so they can focus on the more important courses in their major. Interestingly enough, however, that's not the kind of rhetoric one hears from employers. A survey of business executives in America revealed that 67 percent of them preferred college graduates who either had a well-rounded education focusing on broad knowledge and skills, or an undergraduate program that combined broad knowledge with training in a specific field. Only 22 percent endorsed an undergraduate program that focused solely on education in a specific field. As one executive remarked, "I look for people who take accountability, responsibility, and are good team people over anything else. I can teach the technical."

The features of a global and creative world should make it clear how shortsighted "getting general education out of the way" is, and why employers want graduates with a balanced education. The liberal arts are designed to nurture the qualities of mind that are essential in a global age. For example, the study of literature develops an awareness of narrative, the ability to read critically and insightfully, and the ability to see the world from other perspectives. The study of politics develops a sense of power structures, an awareness of group interactions, and an awareness of how institutions function that may become valuable in a corporate job someday.

> *The liberal arts are designed to nurture the qualities of mind that are essential in a global age.*

This is not to say you should become an art history major if you want to be CEO of Microsoft—nor that you should drop out of college altogether as Bill Gates did. But even students who major in highly specialized disciplines such as engineering need to take the liberal arts seriously. That point was expressed in "Holistic Engineering," an insightful article by Domenico Grasso, dean of the College of Engineering at the University of Vermont, and David Martinelli, chair of the department of engineering at West Virginia

University. Because technology is becoming ever more complex and "increasingly embedded in the human experience," they observe, engineers need to think beyond the narrow bounds of their discipline. "A new kind of engineer is needed," they write, "one who can think broadly across disciplines and consider the human dimensions that are at the heart of every design challenge." In a world where applied technology can be outsourced, they argue, today's engineers need to find their niche as innovative problem *definers*, not just technical problem solvers. Their conclusion: engineers need to develop the ability to think "powerfully and critically in many other disciplines."

If in today's economy even engineers need a broad liberal arts education, the same is certainly true of lawyers, economists, teachers, and graphic designers. General education is not something to get out of the way but is essential to an effective undergraduate education. As David Epstein concludes in *Range: Why Generalists Will Triumph in a Specialized World*, "As technology spins the world into vaster webs of interconnected systems in which each individual only sees a small part, we need more generalists: people who start broad and embrace diverse experiences and perspectives while they progress."

Go Global

In today's increasingly flat world, one trait that ranks high on the list of desirable qualities is the ability to understand and collaborate effectively with people from different cultures. Even college graduates who never plan to venture outside the United States will have to function cross-culturally in the American economy. Given current demographic trends, the US Census Bureau predicts that the United States will be a "minority culture" by the year 2045. That is, in a few decades no single ethnic group will comprise a majority of the population, as whites currently do. Moreover, the ability to function cross-culturally is not something one learns by sitting in a classroom and reading a book about a different culture. You have to get out there and experience the culture. That's why a cross-cultural study abroad program is one of the most valuable experiences that students report when they graduate. Eighty-three percent of college graduates who studied abroad during their undergraduate years rated the experience as having a significant impact on their lives, higher than their responses for both classroom work and college friendships.

The most valuable undergraduate education, therefore, includes some significant time of study in another culture. There is simply no substitute for the experience of getting in a boat or an airplane and arriving in a world where the signs are unreadable, the food is strange, and you are challenged to understand and communicate with people who see the world differently than you do. Cross-cultural study provides an incredible opportunity to learn new things, but it also provides a mirror on your culture and prods you to question your own beliefs and perspective. Indeed, foreign travel is one of the best ways we learn to adjust and broaden our own Christian worldview. G. K. Chesterton once remarked the purpose of travel is not simply to set foot on foreign land: "It is at last to set foot on one's *own* country as a foreign land." That's why of all the disruptions to higher education brought about by COVID-19, one of the saddest was the premature conclusion of a study abroad experience for thousands of college students forced to return home early. And it's why continuing to support overseas study amid global instability needs to be a top priority for college leaders.

Because it takes time to learn a new culture, the ideal cross-cultural experience is a full semester studying abroad. Most Christian colleges provide ample opportunities to spend a semester studying in China, Italy, Ecuador, or another part of the world. Many students, however, cannot spend an entire semester away from their home university. Fortunately, research indicates that, if done well, even a short-term study abroad experience has a significant educational impact. In fact, a survey of college graduates indicated that students who stud-

> *There is simply no substitute for the experience of getting in a boat or an airplane and arriving in a world where the signs are unreadable, the food is strange, and you are challenged to understand and communicate with people who see the world differently than you do.*

ied abroad for four weeks or less were just as likely to be globally engaged as students who spent a semester abroad. Moreover, short-term study abroad programs abound at Christian colleges, either during the summer months, in a January term, or both.

In sum, an education that lasts well beyond your college years is one that prepares you not only to think holistically and creatively but also enables you to think globally and function cross-culturally.

"The world is a book," Augustine said, "and those who do not travel read only a page."

All this discussion of the practical benefits of a liberal arts education may seem inconsistent with the previous chapters' discussion of the Christian foundations of education. But there's no reason a Christian liberal arts education cannot be both intrinsically good and also beneficial practically. When I was a child, Campbell's ran a marketing campaign designed to appeal both to children and to their parents. "Campbell's soup is not just good," the slogan went. "It's good *for* you." We can think of a Christian liberal arts education in the same way. Because of the doctrine of Creation, learning is intrinsically good. God created the world, and he created humans in his own image to understand his Creation, to delight in it, and to develop it in new and creative ways. Education is also good because, as God's people in a fallen world, we become more effective coredeemers with God when we have the skills and insights that a college education provides.

But being intrinsically good doesn't mean that a college education cannot also be good *for* you. Because God is the Creator of all things, at some level "good" and "good for you" become virtually inseparable. Physical health, for example, is good for its own sake, but it's also the case that a healthy person is generally able to accomplish more in life than an unhealthy person. Similarly, the intrinsically good insights and skills we acquire as God's image bearers also prepare us to function effectively in a global economy where creativity, critical thinking, teamwork, and cross-cultural agility are vital qualities. A robust, globally focused Christian education rooted in the liberal arts is truly good *and* good for you.

A Note on Sources

Thomas Friedman's comments on higher education are found in Jeffrey Selingo, "Rethinking Higher Education for a Changing World," *Chronicle of Higher Education* (July 12, 2006). The history of the liberal arts is found in Cornelius Plantinga, *Engaging God's World* (Grand Rapids: Eerdmans, 2002), 191–97. Two good sources on the Conceptual Age are Scott Hartley, *The Fuzzy and the Techie* (Boston: Mariner, 2017), and Daniel Pink, *A Whole New Mind: Why Right-Brainers Will Rule the Future* (New York: Riverhead, 2005).

Data on college graduate earnings by major is found in many sources and summarized in Scott Carlson, "Over Time, Humanities Grads Close the Pay Gap with Professional Peers," *Chronicle of Higher Education* (February 7, 2018). The survey of Fortune 500 CEOs was published in "Offbeat Majors Help CEOs Think outside the Box," *USA Today*, July 24, 2001. The survey of business executives is in Peter D. Hart Research Associates, "How Should Colleges Prepare Students to Succeed in Today's Global Economy?" (white paper on behalf of the Association of American Colleges and Universities, 2006). Observations on the importance of liberal arts for students who major in highly specialized disciplines such as engineering are in Grasso and Martinelli, "Holistic Engineering," *Chronicle of Higher Education* (March 16, 2007). Another helpful book on this topic is David Epstein, *Range: Why Generalists Triumph in a Specialized World* (New York: Riverhead, 2019).

The survey of study abroad students is found in Karin Fischer, "Short Study-Abroad Trips," *Chronicle of Higher Education* (February 20, 2009). G. K. Chesterton's quote is from his work *Tremendous Trifles* (New York: Dodd and Mead, 1920), 245–46.

Questions for Reflection and Discussion

1. Should Christian colleges prescribe a set list of required "core" classes, or give students flexibility to choose their own courses? Why?

2. What liberal arts courses, if any, do you think should be required by a Christian college? Why?

3. What would the notion of "creativity, not just computation" look like in your field of study or intended career?

4. Why would a person need to learn to think holistically in a field such as business or education? Any examples?

5. Why is cross-cultural study important in today's world? What sort of experience or program would relate best to your interests or major?

8 YOUR COLLEGE YEARS AND BEYOND

Living Counterculturally as a College Student

WE began this book with a story about water—David Foster Wallace's opening joke about the fish asking his friend, "What the heck is water?" The point was that we swim in a cultural water of assumptions, behaviors, and expectations that we rarely notice and usually just take for granted.

Now let me extend that analogy. Actually, the cultural water we swim in is not a pond but a stream. If you have ever ridden an inner tube down a gently flowing river, you've experienced this sensation: when you look down at the water your toes are dipped in, it seems as if you're motionless. But then you raise your eyes and look at the river bank, and you realize the river is carrying you, quietly and imperceptibly, in a particular direction. That's what our culture is like—not just a college culture, as we saw in Chapter One, but our broader culture as well. Whether we notice it or not, we're steadily being pushed in a certain direction—to live and think in certain ways. And while some of these influences may be neutral or even positive, others are antithetical both to our college experience and to our lives as thoughtful, faithful Christians.

> *Whether we notice it or not, we're steadily being pushed in a certain direction— to live and think in certain ways. And while some of these influences may be neutral or even positive, others are antithetical both to our college experience and to our lives as thoughtful, faithful Christians.*

Christian philosopher James K. A. Smith observes that our culture promotes certain "scripts" that form us into certain roles over time—roles like student, worker, shopper, soccer player, and consumer. They're not necessarily bad roles, but they're not necessarily good ones, either, and sometimes they go against the grain of the stories God would have us live. That's why in his letter to the Romans, the apostle Paul writes, "Do not conform to the pattern of this world, but be transformed by the renewing of your mind. Then you will be able to test and approve what God's will is" (Rom. 12:2). As Christians, we're called to recognize that our surrounding culture forms us to think, feel, and act in certain ways, and sometimes we need to paddle against the current.

Entire books have been written about the relationship between Christians and culture, but for our purposes, I will focus on two cultural influences that are particularly relevant in our time and place and how they can prevent you from gaining the most from your Christian college. And we'll explore what it means to paddle against the stream as a student and a Christian.

Living Simply in a Culture of Distraction

Countless scholars have described a "culture of distraction" that characterizes modern society. If you've grown up with a smartphone and an Instagram account, as is likely the case, you probably don't need this phenomenon described to you, but here's a summary.

We live in a culture of technology that seeks to grab our attention and fragment it. For example, in 2019, the average American sent and received ninety-four text messages per day. The amount of information we are bombarded with and that we send out increases every year. The problem is, the available minutes per day don't change. The result is that the "information density," if you will, of our lives increases steadily.

> *The amount of information we are bombarded with and that we send out increases every year. The problem is, the available minutes per day don't change.*

I travel frequently, and it seems that airports have a vested interest in bombarding travelers with as much information as possible over TV monitors. The Internet abounds with clickbait—those alluring images that catch your attention—and thanks to the wonders of analytics, advertisers know exactly what kind of worm will hook you (mine happens to be extreme-mountain-biking videos).

Many writers have studied the effect of this information overload on humans. We've grown accustomed to what we call multitasking. Computers run with several windows open and operations running at once, so we assume our brains can do the same. Unfortunately, humans can only do one thing consciously at once, so we actually engage in rapid task *switching* rather than multitasking as computers do. As the volume of information bombarding us increases, so too does the frantic rate of task switching that we require from our brains.

The culture of distraction impacts college life both academically and spiritually. First, neuroscience is revealing that our brains are a lot like muscles: they develop in the direction of their use. We all know that if you exercise a certain part of the body, it will gradually strengthen and grow. Take, for example, a professional tennis player, whose "tennis" arm is typically larger than the other arm. Or a professional cyclist with massive thighs and pencil-thin arms.

It's not as obvious, but a similar phenomenon happens with our brains. Neuron pathways that get used frequently are strengthened and widened, while pathways that don't get used deteriorate. As computer science professor Cal Newport explains in his book *Deep Work*, when we allow our minds to shift from one thing to another every half minute, we prevent our brains from developing the channels needed for sustained attention. We lose the ability to focus on a specific thing for an extended period of time. And that's a problem, because as I'm sure you noticed when writing a paper or studying for an exam, good work requires sustained, focused attention—what Newport calls "deliberative practice." But our culture of distraction makes such focused attention increasingly difficult.

For Christian college students, however, there's a deeper problem with our culture of distraction. As humans, our attention is naturally drawn to motion, sound, and color—the sorts of stimuli that our electronic devices provide. But Christianity is a religion of the still, the quiet, and the unseen. This theme is throughout the Bible, but there is a particularly vivid example in the story of the Old Testament prophet Elijah, in which Elijah recognizes God's presence not in the loud and dramatic but in a gentle whisper.

> The LORD said, "Go out and stand on the mountain in the presence of the LORD, for the LORD is about to pass by." Then a great and powerful wind tore the mountains apart and shattered the rocks before the LORD, but the LORD was not in the wind. After the wind there was an earthquake, but the LORD was not in the earthquake. After the earthquake came a fire, but the LORD was not in the fire. And after the fire came a gentle whisper. When Elijah heard it, he pulled his cloak over his face and went out and stood at the mouth of the cave. (1 Kings 19:11–13)

So how does one hear a gentle whisper? Obviously, by being quiet and sitting still, which is why Psalm 46:10 says, "Be still, and know that I am God." Hearing God requires that we learn to be still and quiet, which is the very thing our culture of distraction seeks to keep us from doing.

Unfortunately, college campuses, even Christian ones, are not exactly oriented toward cultivating a sense of

Hearing God requires that we learn to be still and quiet, which is the very thing our culture of distraction seeks to keep us from doing.

quiet and reflection. Not only are there the standard five courses in a regular semester, but those are typically topped with a generous helping of cultural events, religious activities, intramural sports, late-night gatherings, and for many students, a part-time job. So how do we cultivate a sense of simplicity and calm amid college life? Not by willpower but by *practice*; in other words, by creating some daily routines of simplicity and intentionality amid the hectic pace of college life. Such routines will look different for each person, but here are a few simple suggestions.

First, take some time at the beginning of each day away from your phone and computer—not because they're evil but because our brains, and souls, need to be rewired to think deeply and to pay attention to the quieter things in life. Pastor and author Tish Warren, in her insightful book *Liturgy of the Ordinary*, describes changing her morning routine:

> At that time my typical morning routine was that shortly after waking I'd grab my smartphone. Like digital caffeine, it would prod my foggy brain into coherence and activity. Before getting out of bed, I'd check my email, scroll through the news, glance at Facebook or Twitter. My morning smartphone ritual was brief—no more than five or ten minutes. But my day was imprinted by technology. Without realizing it, I had slowly built a habit: a steady resistance to and dread of boredom.

Warren developed a new routine upon waking up of making her bed and sitting on her bed in silence for a few minutes before launching into her day and her devices. She continues:

My new routine didn't make me wildly successful or cheerfully buoyant as some had promised, but I began to notice, very subtly, that my day was imprinted differently. The first activity of my day, the first move I made, was not that of a consumer, but that of a co-laborer with God. Instead of going to a device for a morning fix of instant infotainment, I touched the tangible softness of our well-worn covers, tugged against wrinkled cotton, felt the hard wood beneath my bare feet. In the creation story, God entered chaos and made order and beauty. In making my bed I reflected that creative act in the tiniest, most ordinary way. In my small chaos, I made small order.

Obviously, the details of a morning routine will vary for each individual, and if you share a shoebox-sized dorm room with a roommate, your Zen-like reflections on your made bed might be interrupted by the sound of toothbrushing ten feet away. The point is to develop and maintain a sensible way to begin your day quietly with yourself and God, not with a device. If we're not intentional about controlling our devices, then it's likely that our devices will end up controlling us.

If we're not intentional about controlling our devices, then it's likely that our devices will end up controlling us.

Second, develop a healthy rhythm of work and rest. Such a rhythm was easier for earlier generations, when work was an actual place—whether a field, a factory, or an office building.

When you left the place, you left the work. College is different. Term papers and lab reports don't exist in a particular place. Like much of modern work, college work is a *concept*—a disembodied, portable activity—and our technology makes that work as portable as possible. The blessing of being able to sit at the beach while working on your laptop becomes the curse of, well, working on your laptop while you're at the beach. Thus, we need to create virtual fences around our work to hem it in. One of the benefits of a college campus is that it provides plenty of outlets to get your mind away from academic work and refresh your soul, whether that's intramural sports, weekend outings, or social activities.

Third, get outside and be active every day. Our bodies were designed for motion. Walking, for example, keeps us in touch with the pace and rhythm of nature. Jesus walked about three thousand miles during his years of ministry; many of his deepest conversations with his disciples occurred when they were walking the dusty roads of Palestine. Philosopher Søren Kierkegaard wrote, "Every day, I walk myself into a state of well-being and walk away from every illness. I have walked myself into my best thoughts, and I know of no thought so burdensome that one cannot walk away from it." College life has more than its share of stresses and distractions, and regular time outside in nature—away from our phones and computers—can reorient our minds and rebuild our ability for focus and reflection.

Fourth, keep a regular journal. One doesn't have to write in it every day or try to record every event, but living intentionally as Christians means seeing our lives as stories and noticing the plot the story is taking. The value of keeping a journal is that it forces you to step out of yourself and your daily life and view it from the balcony, as it were. It develops a habit of seeing your life as a story taking shape above the clutter and busyness of daily life.

We live in a culture that keeps us distracted with emails, texts, newsfeeds, and thoughts of tomorrow, next week, and next year. In this culture, Christ calls us to turn down the volume so we can hear his gentle whisper amid the noise. The college years are an important time to develop habits that will enable you to live simply in a culture of distraction.

> *Living intentionally as Christians means seeing our lives as stories and noticing the plot the story is taking.*

Living Together in a Culture of Isolation

There's a second way in which the river of modern culture works against a meaningful college experience. Not only do we live in a culture of *distraction*; we also live in a culture of *isolation* in which the practice of real community is increasingly difficult.

As we all know, it's possible to be with other people but still be profoundly alone. In fact, our culture of technology has made it possible to be, as author Sherry Turkle puts it, "alone together." In a world of constant connection on the Internet, virtual relationships through texts and images can come to replace real ones. Relationships mediated through a device are safer and more manageable than dealing with real people in real time. Turkle writes, "When one becomes accustomed to virtual companionship without demands, life with people may seem overwhelming." We put

> *We also live in a culture of isolation in which the practice of real community is increasingly difficult.*

our perfect selves on Facebook and Instagram and comment on and like other people's experiences. As the number of texts and images grows, so does our sense of inadequacy and isolation from real people. What Google Maps has done to our ability to read maps, Instagram is doing to our ability to carry on meaningful conversations.

Like the culture of distraction, the culture of isolation is harmful to a Christian college because as Christians, we are deeply formed in community—not just intellectually, as we saw in Chapter One, but spiritually and morally as well. That's why when Paul urged his fellow Christ followers to be transformed, he was not writing to an individual but to a community—*Romans* in the plural—that is, being transformed as a group, not as a random collection of individuals. Romans 12 begins with the phrase, "I urge you, *brothers and sisters*." From the early centuries on, Christians have understood that if they're going to live counterculturally, they need to live in community.

Much of the power of a Christian college, therefore, derives from its nature as a learning *community*—which makes it even more important to make the most of college by being intentional about resisting the culture of isolation and engaging in real community. God has designed human beings for real, authentic relationships. Our souls know the difference between a text conversation with emoticons and a real conversation over coffee. So how are we to live together in a culture of isolation? Here are some suggestions for college students.

First, take advantage of the opportunities for real, intentional, unmediated community that exist at a Christian college—opportunities that may be less accessible in the postcollege years. Of course, students often complain about the Christian college "bubble," but it doesn't have to be that way. We can envision the Christian college as a football huddle rather than an isolated bubble: the purpose of gathering in community is to be more effective at engaging in society. The healthy Christian life consists of a rhythm of time together and time in the world. We huddle up, call a

Much of the power of a Christian college, therefore, derives from its nature as a learning community—which makes it even more important to make the most of college by being intentional about resisting the culture of isolation and engaging in real community.

play, put our hands together, run the play, and then regather to call another play. But it's helpful to keep in mind that you will most likely have several decades' worth of time to function "out there" in the world, and a few years of intentional, close Christian community can be a valuable thing.

Second, take advantage of one of the most valuable features of a Christian college: the opportunity to develop meaningful relationships with Christian professors. Such individuals choose to work

> *We can envision the Christian college as a football huddle rather than an isolated bubble: the purpose of gathering in community is to be more effective at engaging in society.*

at a Christian college because they are called not only to teach courses and write books, but also to have a personal influence on students. That may involve summoning the courage to visit a professor during office hours or asking a professor to direct a thesis project. Developing such relationships not only positions you well for a job or graduate school in a society in which professional references are crucial, but it can have a lasting impact on your life, as I can attest from experience.

Third, develop a healthy rhythm of friendship, community, and solitude—something that is especially important on a resident college campus. We all need appropriate amounts of each, and we need to know ourselves well enough to know which we need to emphasize more. German theologian Dietrich Bonhoeffer summarized this well when he wrote:

> Let him who cannot be alone beware of community. . . . Let him who is not in community beware of being alone. . . . Each by itself has profound perils and pitfalls. One who wants fellowship without solitude plunges into the void of words and feelings, and the one who seeks solitude without fellowship perishes in the abyss of vanity, self-infatuation and despair.

It's not about replacing our natural tendencies but simply developing a balance. We all need times of solitude, one-on-one times with close friends, and times in community. Part of developing a healthy Christian life is learning to keep each of them in balance.

Finally, avoid the cultural monotony of life lived entirely with other college students by involving yourself in a local church. According to the Bible, we're Christians not simply by believing certain things about God and the world, but because we *participate in a community* that lives in a particular—and at times a peculiar—way. The community is called the church. And like

> *We all need times of solitude, one-on-one times with close friends, and times in community. Part of developing a healthy Christian life is learning to keep each of them in balance.*

our families, our fellow church members are not always people of our age and our choosing. A few years ago, my wife and I were living in downtown Washington, DC, and we attended a church in our neighborhood. Every week in church we sang the Doxology after the offering. There was an elderly gentleman who came by himself each week. At the end of the Doxology, he would cup his hands around his mouth and play the "Amen" by blowing into his hands like a trumpet. He also managed to sit right in front of me every week (or so it seemed).

I probably wouldn't choose to friend this person on Facebook, or invite him to the local pub for pints on Thursday night. But every

Sunday morning I would shake his hand and ask him how his week was, and he would ask my wife and me how we were doing. That's the value of local churches as opposed to virtual communities: we don't choose who we interact with, but God does. And being exposed to people opens us up beyond our little world and limited realm of experience.

I have employed several water metaphors in this book—whether that's young fish swimming obliviously in water, or floating down a river on an inner tube. So let me conclude with one more. At our cottage up north on a small lake, I like to lie on my paddleboard and paddle with my hands into the wind out to the middle of the lake. Eventually, I stop paddling and let the wind push me back to the shore. Because the fin is in the back of the board, when I stop pad-

> *The value of a Christian college, then, is not simply that it sets us on a path toward thinking more Christianly (though hopefully it does that), but that it forms us to live a different way.*

dling and lose speed, at some point the wind will push the nose of my board around and the entire board will rotate 180 degrees to drift with the wind. The interesting thing is that the direction the nose of the board moves—either to the right or the left—is predetermined by the slight, imperceptible angle of the board toward the wind when I stop paddling.

For many of us, the college years play a similar role in our lives. We may not notice at the time, but the attitudes, habits, inclinations, and relationships we develop in college significantly influence the direction of our lives. The value of a Christian college, then, is not simply that it sets us on a path toward thinking more Christianly (though hopefully it does that), but that it forms us to *live* a different way. We don't just drift serenely down a river on an inner tube; rather, we recognize the important ways in which our culture works against genuine Christianity and paddle upstream instead. In a culture of distraction and busyness, we can orient ourselves toward simplicity and intentionality in order to hear God's quiet voice. In a culture of isolation, we can develop authentic relationships that will continue to form us throughout our lives. At its best, a Christian college sets us on a path toward developing keen minds and flourishing lives that honor God and bless the world around us.

A Note on Sources

A number of insightful books have been written in recent years, both from Christian and secular perspectives, on modern culture and the impact of technology. Some of the best are Matthew Crawford, *The World beyond Your Head: On Becoming an Individual in an Age of Distraction* (New York: Farrar, Strauss, and Geroux, 2015); Cal Newport, *Deep Work: Rules for Focused Living in a Distracted World* (New York: Grand Central, 2016); and Jean Twenge, *iGen: Why Today's Super-Connected Kids Are Growing Up Less Rebellious, More Tolerant, Less Happy—and Completely Unprepared for Adulthood—and What That Means for the Rest of Us* (New York: Atria Books, 2017). Also still relevant is Nicholas Carr, *The Shallows: What the Internet Is Doing to Our Brains* (New York: W. W. Norton, 2010).

Three important books on Christian formation and living in a technological age are Andy Crouch, *The Tech-Wise Family: Everyday Steps for Putting Techology in Its Place* (Ada, MI: Baker Books, 2017); James K. A. Smith, *You Are What You Love: The Spiritual Power of Habit* (Ada, MI: Brazos Press, 2016); and Tish Warren, *The Liturgy of the Ordinary: Sacred Practices in Everyday Life* (Downers Grove, IL: InterVarsity Press, 2019).

Three books that explore issues of community are Dietrich Bonhoeffer, *Life Together* (Philadelphia: Fortress Press, 2015); Rod Dreher, *The Benedict Option: A Strategy for Christians in a Post-Christian Nation* (New York: Sentinel, 2017); and Sherry Turkle, *Alone Together: Why We Expect More from Technology and Less from Each Other* (New York: Basic Books, 2017).

Questions for Reflection and Discussion

1. If cultural influences are often difficult to notice, how does one go about discovering them? Are there additional ways that our surrounding culture influences us?

2. Is it really possible to cultivate habits of simplicity and reflection during the college years? Why or why not?

3. Why do you think God chooses to make himself known in stillness and quiet?

4. What practices of community would make sense for you to cultivate as a college student?

5. If it's really the case that the college years are so influential, how would—or should—that affect how you approach your time in college?